Landmark
American Speeches

Volume I : The 17th and 18th Centuries

Maureen Harrison & Steve Gilbert
Editors

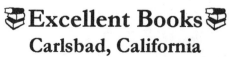

Excellent Books
Carlsbad, California

EXCELLENT BOOKS
Post Office Box 131322
Carlsbad, CA 92013-1322

Publisher's Cataloging in Publication Data

Landmark American Speeches, Volume I: The 17th and 18th Centuries/ Maureen Harrison, Steve Gilbert, editors.
    p. cm. - (Landmark Speeches Series)
Bibliography: p.

1. Speeches, addresses, etc., American.
I. Title. II. Harrison, Maureen. III. Gilbert, Steve.
IV. Series: Landmark Speeches Series.

PN6122. L235 2001   LC 98-72975
815.508 L235 -dc20
ISBN 1-880780-16-X

Introduction

Eloquence is the power to translate a truth into language perfectly intelligible to the people to whom you speak.

- Ralph Waldo Emerson

Landmark American Speeches is a collection of outstanding American eloquence, plainly spoken public words, that allows readers to *hear* from those unforgettable men and women who have made our history.

The first volume of this collection, *Landmark American Speeches: The 17ᵗʰ and 18ᵗʰ Centuries,* presents twenty-three timeless speeches. Each speech is placed in its correct historic context by a complete biography of the speaker, a history of the speech, and a bibliography of the event.

In *Give Me Liberty Or Give Me Death!* Patrick Henry electrifies colonial America with a call to revolution - *I know not what course others may take but, as for me, give me liberty or give me death!* In *These Are The Times That Try Men's Souls,* Thomas Paine's immortal words are read to the Continental Army - *These are the times that try men's souls. The summer soldier and the sunshine patriot will, in this crisis, shrink from the service of their country.* In *The Signing Of The Constitution,* Benjamin Franklin urges his fellow delegates to ratify the proposed U.S. Constitution - *I cannot help expressing a wish that every member of the Constitutional Convention who may still have objections to it would with me on this occasion doubt a little of his own infallibility and put his name to this instrument.* In his *Farewell Address,* President George Washington warns America against dangerous foreign entanglements - *So far as we have formed engagements, let them be fulfilled with perfect good faith. Here let us stop.*

Landmark American Speeches: The 17ᵗʰ and 18ᵗʰ Centuries presents to the readers an unflinching view of American history, contrasting the great spoken words of independence, liberty, freedom, and justice with the ugly words of intolerance, fear, fanaticism, and racism.

International College
Information Resource Center
2655 Northbrooke Drive
Naples, Florida USA 34119
www.internationalcollege.edu

In *The Twelve Tenets Of Conscience*, Roger Williams indicts the Puritans for their intolerance - *The doctrine of persecution for the cause of conscience is proved guilty of all the blood of the souls crying for vengeance under the altar.* In *I Know The Difference Of Peace and War*, Algonquin Chief Powhatan speaks of his fear that a war of racial extermination will be waged against America's native peoples - *I fear you are come to destroy my country.* In *The Heresy Trial Of Anne Hutchinson*, Anne Hutchinson defends herself against the religious persecution from which she had fled - *Take heed how you proceed against me, for I know that for this you go about to do to me, God will ruin you and your posterity.* In *Slave-Keeping*, Benjamin Rush warns prophetically - *Remember that national crimes require national punishments.*

Landmark American Speeches is designed to be an easy-to-use, all-in-one, ready-reference library resource. Most of these speeches have been selected on the basis of either their enduring impact on American government - Thomas Jefferson on the Declaration of Independence, James Madison and Alexander Hamilton on the Constitution - or their lasting imprint on American liberty - William Penn on freedom of speech, Andrew Hamilton on freedom of the press, John Adams on the right to a fair trail. Others - Jonathan Edwards on punishment for sin, and Increase Mather on the dangers of dancing - are included as verbal portraits of the lives and times of past generations of Americans. Once a speech was selected for inclusion in *Landmark American Speeches*, we made every effort to either obtain the original text, or to reconcile differing texts, to provide young adult and general adult readers the authentic words of the speakers. The only change we made to the texts is to carefully edit the essential sections presented into modern spelling and grammar.

Eloquence made Americans listen to these words. The ideas these *Landmark Speeches* contain have made them timeless.

- M.H. & S.G.

Table Of Contents

John Adams
The Boston Massacre Murders
1

If we cannot speak the law as it is, where is our liberty? And this is law, that wherever more than three persons are gathered together to accomplish anything with force, it is a riot.

Samuel Adams
American Independence
20

Courage then, my countrymen, our contest is not only whether we ourselves shall be free, but whether there shall be left to mankind an asylum on earth for civil and religious liberty.

Mary Easty
A "Salem Witch" Pleads For Mercy
37

I know not the least thing of witchcraft.

Jonathan Edwards
Sinners In The Hands Of An Angry God
40

There is nothing between you and hell but the air; it is only the power and mere pleasure of God that holds you up.

Benjamin Franklin
The Signing Of The Constitution
60

I cannot help expressing a wish that every member of the Convention who may still have objections to it would with me on this occasion doubt a little of his own infallibility and, to make manifest our unanimity, put his name to this instrument.

Alexander Hamilton
Republican Government
64

We all, with equal sincerity, profess to be anxious for the establishment of a republican government on a safe and solid basis. It is the object of the wishes of every honest man in the United States.

Andrew Hamilton
The Trial Of John Peter Zenger
74

The loss of liberty to a generous mind is worse than death; and yet we know there have been those in all ages who, for the sake of preferment or some imaginary honor, have freely lent a helping hand to oppress, nay, to destroy, their country.

John Hancock
The Boston Massacre Remembered
82

When Heaven in anger, for a dreadful moment, suffered Hell to take the reins, when Satan with his chosen band opened the sluices of New England's blood, and sacrilegiously polluted our land with the dead bodies of her guiltless sons!

Patrick Henry
Give Me Liberty Or Give Me Death!
96

Is life so dear, or peace so sweet, as to be purchased at the price of chains and slavery? Forbid it, Almighty God! I know not what course others may take, but as for me, give me liberty or give me death!

Anne Hutchinson
The Heresy Trial Of Anne Hutchinson
101

Take heed how you proceed against me, for I know that for this you go about to do to me, God will ruin you and your posterity, and this whole State.

John Jay
Address To The People Of England
105

Can the intervention of the sea that divides us cause disparity in rights, or can any reason be given why English subjects who live three thousand miles from the royal palace should enjoy less liberty than those who are three hundred miles distant from it?

Thomas Jefferson
The First Public Readings Of
The Declaration Of Independence
118

We hold these truths to be self-evident: that all men are created equal, that they are endowed by their Creator with certain unalienable rights, that among these are life, liberty, and the pursuit of happiness.

Henry Lee
The Death Of George Washington
124

First in war, first in peace, first in the hearts of his countrymen.

James Madison
American Government
135

I wish this government may answer the expectation of its friends, and foil the apprehension of its enemies. I hope the patriotism of the people will continue, and be a sufficient guard to their liberties.

Increase Mather
An Arrow Against Mixed Dancing
148

If we consider by whom this practice of promiscuous dancing was first invented, we may well conclude that the admitting of it in such a place as New England will be a thing pleasing to the Devil but highly provoking to the Holy God.

James Otis
A Man's House Is His Castle
154

One of the most essential branches of English liberty is the freedom of one's house. A man's house is his castle, and whilst he is quiet, he is as well guarded as a prince in his castle.

Thomas Paine
These Are The Times That Try Men's Souls
163

These are the times that try men's souls. The summer soldier and the sunshine patriot will, in this crisis, shrink from the service of their country; but he that stands it now deserves the love and thanks of man and woman.

William Penn
Right Against Tyranny
175

If it be just and reasonable for men to do as they would be done by, then no sort of men should invade the liberties and properties of other men, because they would not be served so themselves.

Powhatan, Chief of the Algonquins
I Know The Difference Of Peace and War
183

I fear you are come to destroy my country.

Benjamin Rush
Slave-Keeping
186

Remember that national crimes require national punishments, and without declaring what punishment awaits this evil, you may venture to assure them that it cannot pass with impunity unless God shall cease to be just or merciful.

George Washington
Farewell Address
199

The great rule of conduct for us in regard to foreign nations is, in extending our commercial relations, to have with them as little political connection as possible. So far as we have already formed engagements, let them be fulfilled with perfect good faith. Here let us stop.

Roger Williams
The Twelve Tenets Of Conscience
221

The doctrine of persecution for cause of conscience is proved guilty of all the blood of the souls crying for vengeance under the altar.

John Winthrop
The "Little Speech" On Liberty
225

This liberty you are to stand for, with the hazard (not only of your goods, but) of your lives, if need be.

Chronological Table Of Speeches

1607
Chief Powhatan
I Know The Difference Of Peace and War

1637
Anne Hutchinson
The Heresy Trial of Anne Hutchinson

1644
Roger Williams
The Twelve Tenets Of Conscience

1645
John Winthrop
The "Little Speech" On Liberty

1670
William Penn
Right Against Tyranny

1685
Increase Mather
An Arrow Against Mixed Dancing

1692
Mary Easty
A "Salem Witch" Pleads For Mercy

1735
Andrew Hamilton
The Trial Of John Peter Zenger

1741
Jonathan Edwards
Sinners in the Hands of an Angry God

1761
James Otis
A Man's House Is His Castle

1770
John Adams
The Boston Massacre Murders

1773
Benjamin Rush
Slave-Keeping

1774
John Hancock
The Boston Massacre Remembered

John Jay
Address To The People Of England

1775
Patrick Henry
Give Me Liberty Or Give Me Death!

1776
Thomas Jefferson
*The First Public Readings Of
The Declaration Of Independence*

Samuel Adams
American Independence

Thomas Paine
These Are The Times That Try Men's Souls

1787
Benjamin Franklin
The Signing Of The Constitution

1788
James Madison
American Government

Alexander Hamilton
Republican Government

1796
George Washington
Farewell Address

1799
Henry Lee
The Death Of George Washington

This book is dedicated with love to

Leo

John Adams
The Boston Massacre Murders
December 3 - 4, 1770

*[The British soldiers,] not having the fear of God before their eyes,
but being moved and seduced by the devil and their own wicked hearts,
did, on the 5th day of March, 1770, with force and arms, feloniously,
willfully, and of malice aforethought [murder five citizens of Boston].*
- The Boston Massacre Murder Indictment

On March 5, 1770, a lone sentry guarding the Boston Customs House was confronted by a mob of protesters. He
called for help and Captain Thomas Preston and seven additional soldiers marched to his side. They stood their
ground as first verbal and then physical abuse was hurled at
them. One soldier was knocked down and his musket fired.
Suddenly all of Preston's soldiers fired. Protesters and by-
standers fell. Crispus Attucks and Samuel Grey were killed
outright and three others were mortally wounded. On
March 13, 1770, Preston and his soldiers were indicted for
murder and pled not guilty. John Adams accepted the unpopular defense of Captain Preston and the soldiers. In his
Diary Adams wrote, *Persons whose lives are at stake ought to have
counsel.*

John Adams was born on October 19, 1735 in Braintree
(now Quincy), Massachusetts to John Adams and Susanna
(Boylston) Adams. He graduated Harvard College in 1755
and was admitted to the bar in 1758.

At the trial of Captain Preston, Adams argued that the soldiers, threatened by and fearful of the mob, had fired without orders. Preston was acquitted. At the trial of the soldiers, Adams argued that, order or no, the soldiers had
acted in self-defense. Their trial began on November 27.
On December 3 and 4, John Adams delivered his closing
arguments to the jury in the Boston Massacre Murder Trial
with this landmark speech.

John Adams

May it please Your Honor, and you, Gentlemen of the Jury, I am for the prisoners at the bar, and shall apologize for it only in the words of the Marquis Beccaria, *If I can but be the instrument of preserving one life, his blessings and tears of transport shall be a sufficient consolation for me for the contempt of all mankind.*

As the prisoners stand before you for their lives, it may be proper to recollect with what temper the law requires we should proceed to this trial. The form of proceeding at their arraignment has discovered that the spirit of the law upon such occasions is conformable to humanity, to common sense and feeling, that it is all benignity and candor. And the trial commences with the prayer of the court, expressed by the clerk, to the Supreme Judge of judges, empires, and worlds, *God send you a good deliverance.*

We find in the rules laid down by the greatest English judges, who have been the brightest of mankind - We are to look upon it as more beneficial that many guilty persons should escape unpunished than one innocent should suffer. The reason is because it is of more importance to the community that innocence should be protected than it is that guilt should be punished, for guilt and crimes are so frequent in the world that all of them cannot be punished; and many times they happen in such a manner that it is not of much consequence to the public whether they are punished or not. But when innocence itself is brought to the bar and condemned, especially to die, the subject will exclaim, *It is immaterial to me whether I behave well or ill, for virtue itself is no security.* And if such a sentiment as this should take place in the mind of the subject, there would be an end to all security whatsoever. I will read the words of the law itself.

The rules I shall produce to you from Lord Chief Justice Hale, whose character as a lawyer, a man of learning and philosophy, and a Christian, will be disputed by nobody living - one of the greatest and best characters the English nation ever produced. His words are these . . . . , *It is always safer to err in acquitting than punishing, on the part of mercy than the part of justice. . . . Where you are doubtful, never act, that is, if you doubt of the prisoner's guilt, never declare him guilty.*

This is always the rule, especially in cases of life. Another rule from the same author, where he says, . . . *[I]t is better five guilty persons should escape unpunished than one innocent person should die.*

. . . . Indeed, this rule is not peculiar to the English law; there never was a system of laws in the world in which this rule did not prevail. It prevailed in the ancient Roman law, and, which is more remarkable, it prevails in the modern Roman law. Even the judges in the Courts of Inquisition, who with racks, burnings, and scourges examine criminals - even there they preserve it as a maxim, that it is better the guilty should escape punishment than the innocent suffer. . . . This is the temper we ought to set out with, and these the rules we are to be governed by. And I shall take it for granted, as a first principle, that the eight prisoners at the bar had better be all acquitted, though we should admit them all to be guilty, than that any one of them should, by your verdict, be found guilty, being innocent.

I shall now consider the several divisions of law under which the evidence will arrange itself.

The action now before you is homicide, that is, the killing of one man by another. The law calls it homicide, but it is not criminal in all cases for one man to slay another. Had the prisoners been on the Plains of Abraham and slain a hundred Frenchmen apiece, the English law would have considered it as a commendable action, virtuous and praiseworthy, so that every instance of killing a man is not a crime in the eye of the law. There are many other instances which I cannot enumerate - an officer that executes a person under sentence of death, etc. So that, gentlemen, every instance of one man's killing another is not a crime, much less a crime to be punished with death. But to descend to more particulars.

The law divides homicide into three branches; the first is *justifiable*, the second *excusable*, and the third *felonious*. Felonious homicide is subdivided into two branches; the first is murder, which is killing with malice aforethought; the second is manslaughter, which is killing a man on a sudden provocation. Here, gentlemen, are four sorts of homicide; and you are to consider whether all the evidence amounts to the first, second, third, or fourth of these heads. The fact was the slaying [of] five unhappy persons that night. You are to consider whether it was justifiable, excusable, or felonious and, if felonious, whether it was murder or manslaughter. One of these four it must be. You need not divide your attention to any more particulars. I shall, however, before I come to the evidence, show you several authorities which will assist you and me in contemplating the evidence before us.

I shall begin with justifiable homicide. If an officer, a sheriff, execute a man on the gallows, draw and quarter him, as in case of high treason, and cut off his head, this is justifiable homicide. It is his duty. So also, gentlemen, the law has planted fences and barriers around every individual; it is a castle round every man's person, as well as his house. As the love of God and our neighbor comprehends the whole duty of man, so self-love and social comprehend all the duties we owe to mankind; and the first branch is self-love, which is not only our indisputable right, but our clearest duty. By the laws of nature, this is interwoven in the heart of every individual. God Almighty, whose law we cannot alter, has implanted it there, and we can annihilate ourselves as easily as root out this affection for ourselves. It is the first and strongest principle in our nature. Justice Blackstone calls it *the primary canon in the law of nature.* That precept of our holy religion which commands us to love our neighbor as ourselves does not command us to love our neighbor better than ourselves, or so well. No Christian divine has given this interpretation. The precept enjoins that our benevolence to our fellow-men should be as real and sincere as our affection to ourselves, not that it should be as great in degree. A man is authorized, therefore, by common sense and the laws of England, as well as those of nature, to love himself better than his fellow-subject. If two persons are cast away at sea, and get on a plank (a case put by Sir Francis Bacon), and the plank is insufficient to hold them both, the one has a right to push the other off to save himself. The rules of the common law, therefore, which authorize a man to preserve his own life at the expense of another's, are not contradicted by any divine or moral law. We talk of liberty and property, but if we cut up the law of self-defense, we cut up the foundations of both; and if we give up this, the rest is of very little value, and therefore this principle must be strictly attended to, for whatsoever the law pronounces in the case of these eight soldiers will be the law to other persons and after ages. All the persons that have slain mankind in this country from the beginning to this day had better have been acquitted than that a wrong rule and precedent should be established.

. . . . The injured person may repel force by force against any who endeavoreth to commit any kind of felony on him or his. Here the rule is, I have a right to stand on my own defense, if you intend to commit felony. If any of the persons made an attack on these soldiers, with an intention to rob them, if it was but to take their hats feloniously, they had a right to kill them on the spot, and had no business to retreat. If a robber meet me in the street and command me to surrender my purse, I have a right to kill him without asking any questions. If a person commit a bare assault on me, this will not justify killing, but if he assault me in such a manner as to discover an intention to kill me, I have a right to destroy him, that I may put it out of his power to kill me. In the case you will have to consider, I do not know there was any attempt to steal from these persons; however, there were some persons concerned who would, probably enough, have stolen, if there had been anything to steal, and many were there who had no such disposition. But this is not the point we aim at. The question is, are you satisfied the people made the attack in order to kill the soldiers? If you are satisfied that the people, whoever they were, made that assault with a design to kill or maim the soldiers, this was such an assault as will justify the soldiers killing in their own defense. Further, it seems to me, we may make another question, whether you are satisfied that their real intention was to kill or maim, or not? If any reasonable man in the situation of one of these soldiers would have had reason to believe, in the time of it, that the people came with an intention to kill him, whether you have this satisfaction now or not in your own minds, they were justifiable, at least excusable, in firing. You and I may be suspicious that the people who made this assault on the soldiers did it to put them to flight, on purpose that they might go exulting about the town afterwards in triumph, but this will not do. You must place yourselves in the situation of Weems and Kilroy - consider yourselves as knowing that the prejudice of the world about you thought you came to dragoon them into obedience, to statutes, instructions, mandates, and edicts, which they thoroughly detested - that many of these people were thoughtless and inconsiderate, old and young, sailors and landsmen, negroes and mulattoes - that they, the soldiers, had no friends about them; the rest were in opposition to them, with all the bells ringing to call the town together to assist the people in King Street, for they knew by that time that there was no fire - the people shouting, huzzaing, and making the mob whistle, as they call it, which, when a boy makes it in the street is no formidable thing, but when made by a multitude is a most hideous shriek, almost as terrible as an Indian yell - the people crying, *Kill them, kill them. Knock them over,* heaving snowballs, oyster shells, clubs, white-birch sticks three inches and a half in diameter; consider yourselves in this situation, and then judge whether a reasonable man in the soldiers' situation would not have concluded they were going to kill him. I believe if I were to reverse the scene, I should bring it home to our own bosoms. Suppose Colonel Marshall when he came out of his own door and saw these grenadiers coming down with swords, etc., had thought it proper to have appointed a military watch; suppose he had assembled Gray and Attucks that were killed, or any other person in town, and appointed them in that situation as a military watch, and there had come from Murray's barracks thirty or forty soldiers with no other arms than snowballs, cakes of ice, oyster shells, cinders, and clubs, and attacked this military watch in this manner; what do you suppose would have been the feelings and reasonings of any of our householders? I confess, I believe they would not have borne one-half of what the witnesses have sworn the soldiers bore, till they had shot down as many as were necessary to intimidate and disperse the rest, because the law does not oblige us to bear insults to the danger of our lives, to stand still with such a number of people around us, throwing such things at us, and threatening our lives, until we are disabled to defend ourselves.

. . . . And it is not only highly agreeable to reason that a man in such circumstances may lawfully kill another, but it seems also to be confirmed by the general tenor of our books, which, speaking of homicide *se defendo* [in self-defense], suppose it done in some quarrel or affray.

. . . . Here every private person is authorized to arm himself; and on the strength of this authority I do not deny the inhabitants had a right to arm themselves at that time for their defense, not for offense. . . .

There is no occasion for the magistrate to read the riot act. In the case before you, I suppose you will be satisfied when you come to examine the witnesses and compare it with the rules of the common law, abstracted from all mutiny acts and articles of war, that these soldiers were in such a situation that they could not help themselves. People were coming from Royal Exchange Lane, and other parts of the town, with clubs and cord-wood sticks. The soldiers were planted by the wall of the Custom House; they could not retreat; they were surrounded on all sides, for there were people behind them as well as before them. There were a number of people in the Royal Exchange Lane; the soldiers

were so near to the Custom House that they could not retreat, unless they had gone into the brick wall of it. I shall
show you presently that all the party concerned in this unlawful design were guilty of what any one of them did; if
anybody threw a snowball it was the act of the whole party;
if any struck with a club or threw a club, and the club had
killed anybody, the whole party would have been guilty of
murder in the law. . . .

In the case here we will take Montgomery, if you please,
when he was attacked by the stout man with a stick, who
aimed it at his head, with a number of people round him
crying out, *Kill them, kill them.* Had he not a right to kill the
man? If all the party were guilty of the assault made by the
stout man, and all of them had discovered malice in their
hearts, had not Montgomery a right . . . to put it out of
their power to wreak their malice upon him? . . . The next
point is this - that in case of an unlawful assembly, all and
every one of the assembly is guilty of all and every unlawful
act committed by any one of that assembly in prosecution
of the unlawful design set out upon.

Rules of law should be universally known, whatever effect
they may have on politics; they are rules of common law,
the law of the land; and it is certainly true that wherever
there is an unlawful assembly, let it consist of many persons
or of a few, every man in it is guilty of every unlawful act
committed by any one of the whole party, be they more or
be they less, in pursuance of their unlawful design. This is
the policy of the law - to discourage and prevent riots, insurrections, turbulence, and tumults.

In the continual vicissitudes of human things, amidst the
shocks of fortune and the whirls of passion that take place
at certain critical seasons, even in the mildest government,

the people are liable to run into riots and tumults. There are Church-quakes and State-quakes in the moral and political world, as well as earthquakes, storms, and tempests in the physical. Thus much, however, must be said in favor of the people and of human nature, that it is a general, if not a universal truth, that the aptitude of the people to mutinies, seditions, tumults, and insurrections, is in direct proportion to the despotism of the government. In governments completely despotic, that is, where the will of one man is the only law, this disposition is most prevalent. In aristocracies next; in mixed monarchies, less than either of the former; in complete republics the least of all, and under the same form of governments as in a limited monarchy, for example, the virtue and wisdom of the administrations may generally be measured by the peace and order that are seen among the people. However this may be, such is the imperfection of all things in this world, that no form of government, and perhaps no virtue or wisdom in the administration, can at all times avoid riots and disorders among the people.

Now, it is from this difficulty that the policy of the law has framed such strong discouragements to secure the people against tumults because, when they once begin, there is danger of their running to such excesses as will overturn the whole system of government. There is the rule from the reverend sage of the law [Lord Chief Justice Hale], so often quoted before, *All present, aiding and assisting, are equally principal with him that gave the stroke whereof the party died. For though one gave the stroke, yet in interpretation of law it is the stroke of every person that was present, aiding and assisting. . . .*

Now, if the party at Dock Square came with an intention only to beat the soldiers, and began to affray with them, and any of them had been accidentally killed, it would have been murder, because it was an unlawful design they came upon. If but one does it they are all considered in the eye of the law guilty; if any one gives the mortal stroke, they are all principals here; therefore there is a reversal of the scene. If you are satisfied that these soldiers were there on a lawful design, and it should be proved any of them shot without provocation, and killed anybody, he only is answerable for it.

. . . . I believe it will not be hereafter disputed by anybody that this law ought to be known to every one who has any disposition to be concerned in an unlawful assembly. Whatever mischief happens in the prosecution of the design they set out upon, all are answerable for it. It is necessary we should consider the definitions of some other crimes as well as murder; sometimes one crime gives occasion to another. An assault is sometimes the occasion of manslaughter, sometimes of excusable homicide. It is necessary to consider what is a riot. I shall give you the definition of it [according to Lord Chief Justice Hawkins], *Wheresoever more than three persons use force or violence, for the accomplishment of any design whatever, all concerned are rioters.*

Were there not more than three persons in Dock Square? Did they not agree to go to King Street, and attack the main guard? Where, then, is the reason for hesitation at calling it a riot? If we cannot speak the law as it is, where is our liberty? And this is law, that wherever more than three persons are gathered together to accomplish anything with force, it is a riot.

. . . . If we strip ourselves free from all military laws, mutiny acts, articles of war and soldiers' oaths, and consider these prisoners as neighbors - if any of their neighbors were attacked in King Street, they had a right to collect together to suppress this riot and combination. If any number of persons meet together at a fair or market, and happen to fall together by the ears, they are not guilty of a riot, but of a sudden affray. . . .

It would be endless, as well as superfluous, to examine whether every particular person engaged in a riot were in truth one of the first assembly or actually had a previous knowledge of the design thereof. I have endeavored to produce the best authorities, and to give you the rules of law in their words, for I desire not to advance anything of my own. I choose to lay down the rules of law from authorities which cannot be disputed. Another point is this, whether and how far a private person may aid another in distress. Suppose a press-gang should come on shore in this town and assault any sailor or householder in King Street, in order to carry him on board one of his Majesty's ships, and impress him without any warrant as a seaman in his Majesty's service; how far do you suppose the inhabitants would think themselves warranted by law to interpose against that lawless press-gang? I agree that such a press-gang would be as unlawful an assembly as that was in King Street. If they were to press an inhabitant and carry him off for a sailor, would not the inhabitants think themselves warranted by law to interpose in behalf of their fellow-citizen? Now, gentlemen, if the soldiers had no right to interpose in the relief of the sentry, the inhabitants would have no right to interpose with regard to the citizen, for whatever is law for a soldier is law for a sailor and for a citizen. They all stand upon an equal footing in this respect. I believe we shall not have it disputed that it would be lawful to go into King Street and help an honest man there against the pressmaster. We have many instances in the books which authorize it.

Now, suppose you should have a jealousy in your minds that the people who made this attack upon the sentry had nothing in their intention more than to take him off his post, and that was threatened by some. Suppose they intended to go a little further, and tar and feather him, or to ride him . . . , he would have had a good right to have stood upon his defense - the defense of his liberty; and if he could not preserve that without the hazard of his own life, he would have been warranted in depriving those of life who were endeavoring to deprive him of his. That is a point I would not give up for my right hand - nay, for my life.

Well, I say, if the people did this, or if this was only their intention, surely the officers and soldiers had a right to go to his relief; and therefore they set out upon a lawful errand. They were, therefore, a lawful assembly, if we only consider them as private subjects and fellow-citizens, without regard to mutiny acts, articles of war, or soldiers' oaths. A private person, or any number of private persons, has a right to go to the assistance of a fellow-subject in distress or danger of his life, when assaulted and in danger from a few or a multitude.

. . . . If a stranger, a mere fellow-subject, may interpose to defend the liberty, he may, too, defend the life of another individual. But, according to the evidence, some imprudent people, before the sentry, proposed to take him off his post; others threatened his life; and intelligence of this was carried to the main guard before any of the prisoners turned out. They were then ordered out to relieve the sentry; and any of our fellow-citizens might lawfully have gone upon the same errand. They were, therefore, a lawful assembly.

I have but one point of law more to consider, and that is this - In the case before you I do not pretend to prove that every one of the unhappy persons slain was concerned in the riot. . . . [I]t would be endless to prove whether every person that was present and in a riot was concerned in planning the first enterprise or not. Nay, I believe it but justice to say some were perfectly innocent of the occasion. I have reason to suppose that one of them was - Mr. Maverick. He was a very worthy young man, as he has been represented to me, and had no concern in the rioters' proceedings of that night; and I believe the same may be said in favor of one more at least, Mr. Caldwell, who was slain; and, therefore, many people may think that as he and perhaps another was innocent, therefore innocent blood having been shed, that must be expiated by the death of somebody or other. I take notice of this because one gentleman was nominated by the sheriff for a juryman upon this trial, because he had said he believed Captain Preston was innocent, but innocent blood had been shed, and therefore somebody ought to be hanged for it, which he thought was indirectly giving his opinion in this cause. I am afraid many other persons have formed such an opinion. I do not take it to be a rule that where innocent blood is shed the person must die. In the instance of the Frenchmen on the Plains of Abraham, they were innocent, fighting for their king and country; their blood is as innocent as any. There may be multitudes killed, when innocent blood is shed on all sides, so that it is not an invariable rule.

I will put a case in which, I dare say, all will agree with me. Here are two persons, the father and the son, go out a-hunting. They take different roads. The father hears a rushing among the bushes, takes it to be game, fires, and kills his son, through a mistake. Here is innocent blood shed, but yet nobody will say the father ought to die for it. So that the general rule of law is that whenever one person has a right to do an act, and that act, by any accident, takes away the life of another, it is excusable. It bears the same regard to the innocent as to the guilty. If two men are together, and attack me, and I have a right to kill them, I strike at them, and by mistake strike a third and kill him, as I had a right to kill the first, my killing the other will be excusable, as it happened by accident. If I, in the heat of passion, aim a blow at the person who has assaulted me, and aiming at him I kill another person, it is but manslaughter.

. . . . Suppose, in this case, the mulatto man was the person who made the assault; suppose he was concerned in the unlawful assembly, and this party of soldiers, endeavoring to defend themselves against him, happened to kill another person, who was innocent - though the soldiers had no reason, that we know of, to think any person there, at least of that number who were crowding about them, innocent, they might, naturally enough, presume all to be guilty of the riot and assault, and to come with the same design. I say, if on firing on those who were guilty, they accidentally killed an innocent person, it was not their fault. They were obliged to defend themselves against those who were pressing upon them. They are not answerable for it with their lives, for on supposition it was justifiable or excusable to kill Attucks, or any other person, it will be equally justifiable or excusable if in firing at him they killed another, who was innocent; or if the provocation was such as to mitigate the guilt of manslaughter, it will equally mitigate the guilt, if they killed an innocent man undesignedly, in aiming at him who gave the provocation. . . .

I shall now consider one question more, and that is concerning provocation. We have hitherto been considering self-defense, and how far persons may go in defending themselves against aggressors, even by taking away their lives, and now proceed to consider such provocations as the law allows to mitigate or extenuate the guilt of killing, where it is not justifiable or excusable. An assault and battery committed upon a man in such a manner as not to endanger his life is such a provocation as the law allows to reduce killing down to the crime of manslaughter. Now, the law has been made on more considerations than we are capable of making at present; the law considers a man as capable of bearing anything and everything but blows. I may reproach a man as much as I please; I may call him a thief, robber, traitor, scoundrel, coward, lobster, bloody-back, etc., and if he kill me it will be murder, if nothing else but words precede; but if from giving him such kind of language I proceed to take him by the nose, or fillip him on the forehead, that is an assault; that is a blow. The law will not oblige a man to stand still and bear it; there is the distinction. Hands off; touch me not. As soon as you touch me, if I run you through the heart, it is but manslaughter. The utility of this distinction, the more you think of it the more you will be satisfied with it. It is an assault whenever a blow is struck, let it be ever so slight, and sometimes even without a blow. The law considers man as frail and passionate. When his passions are touched, he will be thrown off his guard, and therefore the law makes allowance for this frailty - considers him as in a fit of passion, not having the possession of his intellectual faculties, and therefore does not oblige him to measure out his blows with a yard-stick, or weigh them in a scale. Let him kill with a sword, gun, or hedge-stake, it is not murder, but only manslaughter.

. . . . So that here is the boundary, when a man is assaulted and kills in consequence of that assault, it is but manslaughter. . . .

Every snowball, oyster shell, cake of ice, or bit of cinder, that was thrown that night at the sentinel, was an assault upon him; every one that was thrown at the party of soldiers was an assault upon them, whether it hit any of them or not. I am guilty of an assault if I present a gun at any person; and if I insult him in that manner and he shoots me, it is but manslaughter.

. . . . Insolent, scurrilous, or slanderous language, when it precedes an assault, aggravates it.

[According to Judge Foster,] *We all know that words of reproach, how grating and offensive soever, are in the eye of the law no provocation in the case of voluntary homicide; and yet every man who hath considered the human frame, or but attended to the workings of his own heart, knoweth that affronts of that kind pierce deeper and stimulate in the veins more effectually than a slight injury done to a third person, though under the color of justice, possibly can.*

I produce this to show the assault in this case was aggravated by the scurrilous language which preceded it. Such words of reproach stimulate in the veins and exasperate the mind, and no doubt if an assault and battery succeeds them, killing under such provocation is softened to manslaughter, but killing without such provocation makes it murder.

John Adams

May it please your Honors, and you, Gentlemen of the Jury, I yesterday afternoon produced from the best authorities, those rules of law which must govern all cases of homicide, particularly that which is now before you; it now remains to consider the evidence, and see whether any thing has occurred, that may be compared to the rules read to you; and I will not trouble myself nor you with labored endeavors to be methodical, I shall endeavor to make some few observations, on the testimonies of the witnesses, such as will place the facts in a true point of light, with as much brevity as possible. . . .

The law, in all vicissitudes of government, fluctuations of the passions, or flights of enthusiasm, will preserve a steady undeviating course; it will not bend to the uncertain wishes, imaginations, and wanton tempers of men. To use the words of a great and worthy man, a patriot, and a hero, an enlightened friend of mankind, and a martyr to liberty - I mean Algernon Sidney, who from his earliest infancy sought a tranquil retirement under the shadow of the tree of liberty, with his tongue, his pen, and his sword,

The law (says he) no passion can disturb. 'Tis void of desire and fear, lust and anger. 'Tis . . . written reason, retaining some measure of the divine perfection. It does not enjoin that which pleases a weak, frail man, but without any regard to persons, commands that which is good, and punishes evil in all, whether rich, or poor, high or low. - 'Tis deaf, inexorable, inflexible.

On the one hand it is inexorable to the cries and lamentations of the prisoners; on the other it is deaf, deaf as an adder, to the clamors of the populace.

John Adams

Afterward

The jury deliberated for two and a half hours. They found six of the soldiers *Not Guilty*. Kilroy and Montgomery, the only two soldiers positively identified by witnesses, were found *Guilty of Manslaughter*. The penalty for manslaughter was death. To save their lives, the two soldiers agreed to a punishment based on medieval ecclesiastical law in which a hot poker burned a mark into their thumbs, branding them as convicted criminals.

The verdict of the jury was exactly right. With these words, John Adams summed up the trial that made him famous throughout the thirteen colonies and one of the leading figures of the American Revolution to come. Adams served in the Continental Congresses, taking part in the drafting and signing of the Declaration of Independence. He took part in negotiating the Revolutionary War-ending Treaty of Paris, after which he served as Ambassador to Great Britain. He was twice elected Vice President (1789-1797) and then President (1797-1801). He died on July 4, 1826.

Selected Reading

Adams, Charles Francis, *The Works of John Adams*, 1850.

Adams, John Quincy, and Charles Francis Adams. *The Life of John Adams*, 1856.

Butterfield, L., *The Diary and Autobiography of John Adams*, 1961.

Ferling, John, *John Adams: A Life*, 1992.

Lukes, Bonnie, *The Boston Massacre*, 1998.

Shaw, Peter, *The Character of John Adams*, 1976.

Smith, Page, *John Adams*, 1962.

Wroth, Kinvin, and Hiller Zobel, *The Legal Papers of John Adams*, 1965.

Samuel Adams
American Independence
August 1, 1776

Oh, what a glorious morning for America!
- Samuel Adams, April 19, 1775

The War of American Independence began on April 19, 1775. Samuel Adams' war for American independence had begun long before.

Samuel Adams, Jr. was born in Boston, Massachusetts on September 27, 1722. He was educated at Harvard College. Beginning in 1748, Adams began working for American independence. His friends called him *The Great Propagandist.* His enemies called him *The Great Rabble-Rouser.* He immersed himself in what would become a lifetime of leadership of radical groups, radical politics, radical writing, political resistance to Acts of Parliament, and political street protests. By the mid-1770's Samuel Adams had become the acknowledged leader of the Massachusetts revolutionary movement.

The British ordered his arrest and deportation to England to stand trial for treason. Warned on the night of April 19, 1775 by Paul Revere that the British were marching on Boston to seize the town and take him into custody, Adams fled to Philadelphia. He arrived on May 10, 1775, taking his seat at the Second Continental Congress.

On July 4, 1776, the Declaration of Independence was adopted by the Second Continental Congress. A parchment copy, to be signed by each delegate, was ordered printed. On August 1, 1776, the day before the Declaration was to be officially signed, Samuel Adams delivered this landmark speech at the Pennsylvania State House.

Samuel Adams

Countrymen and brethren, I would have gladly declined an honor to which I find myself unequal. I have not the calmness and impartiality which the infinite importance of this occasion demands. I will not deny the charge of my enemies that resentment for the accumulated injuries of our country and an ardor for her glory, rising to enthusiasm, may deprive me of that accuracy of judgment and expression which men of cooler passions may possess. Let me beseech you, then, to hear me with caution, to examine without prejudice, and to correct the mistakes into which I may be hurried by my zeal.

Truth loves an appeal to the common sense of mankind. Your unperverted understandings can best determine on subjects of a practical nature. The positions and plans which are said to be above the comprehension of the multitude may be always suspected to be visionary and fruitless. He who made all men hath made the truths necessary to human happiness obvious to all.

Our forefathers threw off the yoke of popery in religion; for you is reserved the honor of leveling the popery of politics. They opened the Bible to all, and maintained the capacity of every man to judge for himself in religion. Are we sufficient for the comprehension of the sublimest spiritual truths, and unequal to material and temporal ones? Heaven hath trusted us with the management of things for eternity, and man denies us the ability to judge of the present, or to know from our feelings and experience what will make us happy. *You can discern,* say they, *objects distant and remote, but cannot perceive those within your grasp. Let us have the distribution of present goods, and cut out and manage as you please the interest of futurity.* This day I trust the reign of political protestantism will commence. We have explored the temple of royalty, and found that the idol we have bowed down to has eyes which see not, ears that hear not our prayers, and a heart like the nether millstone. We have this day restored the Sovereign to whom alone men ought to be obedient. He reigns in heaven, and with a propitious eye beholds his subjects assuming that freedom of thought and dignity of self-direction which He bestowed on them. From the rising to the setting sun may his kingdom come.

Having been a slave to the influence of opinions early acquired, and distinctions generally received, I am ever inclined not to despise, but pity, those who are yet in darkness. But to the eye of reason what can be more clear than that all men have an equal right to happiness? Nature made no other distinction than that of higher or lower degrees of power of mind and body. But what mysterious distribution of character has the craft of statesmen, more fatal than priestcraft, introduced! According to their doctrine, the offspring of perhaps the lewd embraces of a successful invader shall, from generation to generation, arrogate the right of lavishing on their pleasures a portion of the fruits of the earth more than sufficient to supply the wants of thousands of their fellow creatures; claim authority to manage them like beasts of burden, and without superior industry, capacity, or virtue, nay, though disgraceful to humanity by their ignorance, intemperance, and brutality, shall be deemed best calculated to frame laws and to consult for the welfare of society.

Were the talents and virtues which Heaven has bestowed on men given merely to make them more obedient drudges, to he sacrificed to the follies and ambitions of a few? Or were not the noble gifts so equally dispensed with a divine purpose and law that they should, as nearly as possible, be equally exerted, and the blessings of Providence be equally enjoyed by all? Away, then, with those absurd systems which, to gratify the pride of a few, debase the greatest part of our species below the order of men. What an affront to the King of the Universe to maintain that the happiness of a monster sunk in debauchery and spreading desolation and murder among men, of a Caligula, a Nero, or a Charles, is more precious in his sight than that of millions of his suppliant creatures who do justice, love mercy, and walk humbly with their God! No, in the judgment of Heaven there is no other superiority among men than a superiority in wisdom and virtue. And can we have a safer model in forming ours? The Deity, then, has not given any order or family of men authority over others; and if any men have given it, they only could give it for themselves. Our forefathers, 'tis said, consented to be subject to the laws of Great Britain. I will not, at present, dispute it, nor mark out the limits and conditions of their submission; but will it be denied that they contracted to pay obedience, and to be under the control of Great Britain because it appeared to them most beneficial in their then present circumstances and situation? We, my countrymen, have the same right to consult and provide for our happiness which they had to promote theirs. If they had a view to posterity in their contracts, it must have been to advance the felicity of their descendants. If they erred in their expectations and prospects we can never be condemned for a conduct which they would have recommended had they foreseen our present condition.

.... No man had once a greater veneration for Englishmen than I entertained. They were dear to me as branches of the same parental trunk, and partakers of the same religion and laws; I still view with respect the remains of the constitution as I would a lifeless body which had once been animated by a great and heroic soul. But when I am roused by the din of arms, when I behold legions of foreign assassins paid by Englishmen to embrue their hands in our blood; when I tread over the uncoffined bones of my countrymen, neighbors, and friends; when I see the locks of a venerable father torn by savage hands, and a feeble mother clasping her infants to her bosom, and on her knees imploring their lives from her own slaves whom Englishmen have allured to treachery and murder; when I behold my country, once the seat of industry, peace, and plenty, changed by Englishmen to a theatre of blood and misery - Heaven forgive me if I cannot root out those passions which it has implanted in my bosom, and detest submission to a people who have either ceased to be human or have not virtue enough to feel their own wretchedness and servitude.

Men who content themselves with the semblance of truth and a display of words, talk much of our obligations to Great Britain for protection. Had she a single eye to our advantage? A nation of shopkeepers are very seldom so disinterested. Let us not be so amused with words. The extension of her commerce was her object. When she defended our coasts she fought for her customers, and convoyed our ship loaded with wealth which we had acquired for her by our industry. She has treated us as beasts of burden, whom the lordly masters cherish that they may carry a greater load. Let us inquire also against whom she has protected us. Against her own enemies with whom we had no quarrel, or only on her account, and against whom we always readily exerted our wealth and strength when they were required. Were these colonies backward in giving assistance to Great Britain when they were called upon, in 1739, to aid the expedition against Carthagena? They at that time sent 3,600 men to join the British army, although the war commenced without their consent.

But the last war, 'tis said, was purely American. This is a vulgar error, which, like many others, has gained credit by being confidently repeated. The dispute between the courts of Great Britain and France related to the limits of Canada and Nova Scotia. The controverted territory was not claimed by any in the colonies, but by the crown of Great Britain. It was therefore their own quarrel. . . .

But what purpose can arguments of this kind answer? Did the protection we received annul our rights as men, and lay us under an obligation of being miserable? Who among you, my countrymen, that is a father, would claim authority to make your child a slave because you had nourished him in his infancy? 'Tis a strange species of generosity which requires a return infinitely more valuable than anything it could have bestowed; that demands, as a reward for a defense of our property, a surrender of those inestimable privileges to the arbitrary will of vindictive tyrants, which alone give value to that very property.

. . . . The Author of Nature directs all his operations to the production of the greatest good, and has made human virtue to consist in a disposition and conduct which tends to the common felicity of his creatures. An abridgment of the natural freedom of man by the institution of political societies is vindicable only on this foot. How absurd, then, is it to draw arguments from the nature of civil society for the annihilation of those very ends which society was intended to procure. Men associate for their mutual advantage. Hence the good and happiness of the members, that is, the majority of the members, of any state, is the great standard by which everything relating to that state must finally be determined. And though it may be supposed that a body of people may be bound by a voluntary resignation (which they have been so infatuated as to make) of all their interests to a single person, or to a few, it can never be conceived that the resignation is obligatory to their posterity, because it is manifestly contrary to the good of the whole that it should be so.

These are the sentiments of the wisest and most virtuous champions of freedom. Attend to a portion on this subject from a book in our defense, written, I had almost said, by the pen of inspiration. *I lay no stress, says he, on charters; they derive their rights from a higher source. It is inconsistent with common sense to imagine that any people would ever think of settling in a distant country on any such condition, or that the people from whom they withdrew should forever be masters of their property and have power to subject them to any modes of government they pleased. And had there been express stipulations to this purpose in all the charters of the colonies they would, in my opinion, be no more bound by them than if it had been stipulated with them that they should go naked or expose themselves to the incursions of wolves and tigers.*

Such are the opinions of every virtuous and enlightened patriot in Great Britain. Their petition to Heaven is *that there may be one free country left upon earth to which they may fly when venality, luxury, and vice shall have completed the ruin of liberty there.*

Courage then, my countrymen! Our contest is not only whether we ourselves shall be free, but whether there shall be left to mankind an asylum on earth for civil and religious liberty. Dismissing, therefore, the justice of our cause as incontestable, the only question is - What is best for us to pursue in our present circumstances?

. . . . We are now on this continent, to the astonishment of the world, three millions of souls united in one common cause. We have large armies, well disciplined and appointed, with commanders inferior to none in military skill, and superior in activity and zeal. We are furnished with arsenals and stores beyond our most sanguine expectations, and foreign nations are waiting to crown our success by their alliances. There are instances of, I would say, an almost astonishing providence in our favor; our success has staggered our enemies, and almost given faith to infidels; so we may truly say it is not our own arm which has saved us. The hand of Heaven appears to have led us on to be, perhaps, humble instruments and means in the great providential dispensation which is completing. We have fled from the political Sodom; let us not look back, lest we perish and become a monument of infamy and derision to the world. For can we ever expect more unanimity and a better preparation for defense, more infatuation of counsel among our enemies, and more valor and zeal among ourselves? The same force and resistance which are sufficient to procure us our liberties will secure us a glorious independence, and support us in the dignity of free, imperial states. We cannot suppose that our opposition has made a corrupt and dissipated nation more friendly to America, or created in them a greater respect for the rights of mankind. We can therefore expect a restoration and establishment of our privileges, and a compensation for the injuries we have received, from their want of power, from their fears, and not from their virtues. The unanimity and valor which will effect an honorable peace can render a future contest for our liberties unnecessary. He who has strength to chain down the wolf is a madman if he lets him loose without drawing his teeth and paring his nails. From the day on which an accommodation takes place between England and America on any other terms than as independent states I shall date the ruin of this country. A political minister will study to lull us into security by granting us the full extent of our petitions. The warm sunshine of influence would melt down the virtue which the violence of the storm rendered more firm and unyielding.

In a state of tranquillity, wealth and luxury our descendants would forget the acts of war and the noble activity and zeal which made their ancestors invincible. Every art of corruption would be employed to loosen the bond of union which renders our resistance formidable. When the spirit of liberty which now animates our hearts and gives success to our arms is extinct, our numbers will accelerate our ruin, and render us easier victims to tyranny. Ye abandoned minions of an infatuated ministry - if peradventure any should yet remain among us - remember that a Warren and Montgomery are numbered among the dead. Contemplate the mangled bodies of your countrymen, and then say what should be the reward of such sacrifices. Bid us and our posterity bow the knee, supplicate the friendship, and plow and sow and reap to glut the avarice of the men who have let loose on us the dogs of war to riot in our blood and hunt us from the face of the earth. If ye love wealth better than liberty, the tranquillity of servitude than the animating contest of freedom, go from us in peace; we ask not your councils or arms. Crouch down and lick the hands which feed you; may your chains set light upon you, and may posterity forget that ye were our countrymen.

To unite the supremacy of Great Britain and the liberty of America is utterly impossible. So vast a continent and at such a distance from the seat of empire, will every day grow more unmanageable. The motion of so unwieldy a body cannot be directed with any dispatch and uniformity without committing to the Parliament of Great Britain powers inconsistent with our freedom. The authority and force which would be absolutely necessary for the preservation of the peace and good order of this continent would put all our valuable rights within the reach of that nation. As the administration of government requires firmer and more numerous supports in proportion to its extent, the burdens imposed on us would be excessive, and we should have the melancholy prospect of their increasing on our posterity. The scale of officers from the rapacious and needy Commissioner to the haughty Governor, and from the Governor with his hungry train, to, perhaps, a licentious and prodigal Viceroy, must be upheld by you and your children. The fleets and armies which will be employed to silence your murmurs and complaints must be supported by the fruits of your industry. And yet with all this enlargement of the expense and powers of government, the administration of it at such a distance, and over so extensive a territory, must necessarily fail of putting the laws into vigorous execution, removing private oppressions and forming plans for the advancement of agriculture and commerce and preserving the vast empire in any tolerable peace and security. If our posterity retain any spark of patriotism they can never tamely submit to such burdens. This country will be made the field of bloody contention till it gains that independence for which nature formed it. It is, therefore, injustice and cruelty to our offspring, and would stamp us with the character of baseness and cowardice, to leave the salvation of this country to be worked out by them with accumulated difficulty and danger.

. . . . This day we are called upon to give a glorious example of what the wisest and best of men were rejoiced to view only in speculation. This day presents the world with the most august spectacle that its annals ever unfolded - millions of freemen deliberately and voluntarily forming themselves into a society for their common defense and common happiness. Immortal spirits of Hampden, Locke, and

Sidney! Will it not add to your benevolent joys to behold your posterity rising to the dignity of men, and evincing to the world the reality and expediency of your systems, and in the actual enjoyment of that equal liberty which you were happy, when on earth, in delineating and recommending to mankind?

Other nations have received their laws from conquerors; some are indebted for a constitution to the sufferings of their ancestors through revolving centuries. The people of this country alone have formally and deliberately chosen a government for themselves, and with open and uninfluenced consent bound themselves into a social compact. Here no man proclaims his birth or wealth as a title to honorable distinction, or to sanctify ignorance and vice with the name of hereditary authority. He who has most zeal and ability to promote public felicity, let him be the servant of the public. This is the only line of distinction drawn by nature. Leave the bird of night to the obscurity for which nature intended him, and expect only from the eagle to brush the clouds with his wings, and look boldly in the face of the sun.

Some who would persuade us that they have tender feelings for future generations, while they are insensible to the happiness of the present, are perpetually foreboding a train of dissensions under our popular system. Such men's reasoning amounts to this - give up all that is valuable to Great Britain, and then you will have no inducement to quarrel among yourselves; or, suffer yourselves to be chained down by your enemies, that you may not be able to fight with your friends. This is an insult on your virtue as well as your common sense. Your unanimity, this day and through the course of the war, is a decisive refutation of such invidious predictions. Our enemies have already had evidence that our present constitution contains in it the justice and ardor of freedom and the wisdom and vigor of the most absolute system. When the law is the will of the people it will be uniform and coherent; but fluctuation, contradiction, and inconsistency of councils must be expected under those governments where every revolution in the ministry of a court produces one in the state, such being the folly and pride of all ministers that they ever pursue measures directly opposite to those of their predecessors. We shall neither be exposed to the necessary convulsions of elective monarchies nor to the want of wisdom, fortitude, and virtue to which hereditary succession is liable. In your hands it will be to perpetuate a prudent, active, and just legislature, and which will never expire till you yourselves lose the virtues which gave it existence.

And, brethren and fellow-countrymen, if it was ever granted to mortals to trace the designs of Providence, and interpret his manifestations in favor of their cause, we may with humility of soul cry out, *Not unto us, not unto us, but to thy name be the praise.* The confusion of the devices among our enemies, and the rage of the elements against them, have done almost as much towards our success as either our councils or our arms. The time at which this attempt on our liberties was made, when we were ripened into maturity, had acquired a knowledge of war, and were free from the incursions of enemies in this country, the gradual advances of our oppressors enabling us to prepare for our defense, the unusual fertility of our lands and clemencies of the seasons, the success which at first attended our feeble arms, producing unanimity among our friends and reducing our internal foes to acquiescence - these are all strong and palpable marks and assurances that Providence is yet gracious unto Zion, that he will turn away the captivity of Jacob.

Our glorious reformers, when they broke through the fetters of superstition, effected more than could be expected from an age so darkened; but they left much to be done by their posterity. They lopped off indeed some of the branches of popery, but they left the root and stock when they left us under the domination of human systems and decisions, usurping the infallibility which can be attributed to revelation alone. They dethroned one usurper only to raise up another; they refused allegiance to the pope only to place the civil magistrate in the throne of Christ, vested with authority to enact laws and inflict penalties in his kingdom. And if we now cast our eyes over the nations of the earth we shall find that, instead of possessing the pure religion of the gospel, they may be divided either into infidels who deny the truth, or politicians who make religion a stalking-horse for their ambition, or professors who walk in the trammels of orthodoxy and are more attentive to traditions and ordinances of men than to the oracles of truth. The civil magistrate has everywhere contaminated religion by making it an engine of policy; and freedom of thought and the right of private judgment in matters of conscience, driven from every other corner of the earth, direct their course to this happy country as their last asylum. Let us cherish the noble guests and shelter them under the wings of a universal toleration. Be this the seat of unbounded religious freedom; she will bring with her in her train industry, wisdom, and commerce. She thrives most when left to shoot forth in her natural luxuriance, and asks from human policy only not to be checked in her growth by artificial encouragements. Thus, by the beneficence of Providence, we shall behold an empire arising, founded on justice and the voluntary consent of the people, and giving full scope to the exercise of those faculties and rights which most ennoble our species.

Besides the advantages of liberty and the most equal constitution, Heaven has given us a country with every variety of climate and soil, pouring forth in abundance whatever is necessary for the support, comfort, and strength of a nation. Within our own borders we possess all the means of sustenance, defense, and commerce; at the same time these advantages are so distributed among the different states of this continent as if nature had in view to proclaim to us - Be united among yourselves and you will want nothing from the rest of the world. The more northern states most amply supply us with every necessary and many of the luxuries of life, with iron, timber, and masts for ships of commerce or of war, with flax for the manufactory of linen, and seed either for oil or exportation. So abundant are our harvests that almost every part raises more than double the quantity of grain requisite for the support of the inhabitants. From Georgia and the Carolinas we have, as well for our own wants as for the purpose of supplying the wants of other powers, indigo, rice, hemp, naval stores, and lumber. Virginia and Maryland teem with wheat, Indian corn, and tobacco. Every nation whose harvest is precarious, or whose lands yield not those commodities which we cultivate, will gladly exchange their superfluities and manufactures for ours.

We have already received many and large cargoes of clothing, military stores, etc., from our commerce with foreign powers; and, in spite of the efforts of the boasted navy of England, we shall continue to profit by this connection. The want of our naval stores has already increased the price of these articles to a great height, especially in Britain. Without our lumber it will be impossible for these haughty Islanders to convey the products of the West Indies to their own ports. For awhile they may, with difficulty, effect it; but without our assistance their resources soon must fail. Indeed, the West India Islands appear as the necessary appendages to this, our empire. They must owe their support to it; and erelong, I doubt not, some of them will, from necessity, wish to enjoy the benefit of our protection. These natural advantages will enable us to remain independent of the world, or make it the interest of European powers to court our alliance and aid in protecting us against the invasion of others. What argument, therefore, do we want to show the equity of our conduct, or motive of interest, to recommend it to our prudence? Nature points out the path, and our enemies have obliged us to pursue it.

If there is any man so base or so weak as to prefer a dependence on Great Britain to the dignity and happiness of living a member of a free and independent nation, let me tell him that necessity now demands what the generous principles of patriotism should have dictated. We have now no other alternative than independence or the most ignominious and galling servitude. The legions of our enemies thicken on our plains. Desolation and death mark their bloody career, whilst the mangled corpses of our countrymen seem to cry out to us as a voice from Heaven,

Will you permit our posterity to groan under the galling chains of our murderers? Has our blood been expended in vain? Is the only reward which our constancy till death has obtained for our country that it should be sunk into a deeper and more ignominious vassalage? Recollect who are the men that demand your submission, to whose decrees you are invited to pay obedience. Men who, unmindful of their relation to you as brethren, of your long, implicit submission to their laws, of the sacrifice which you and your forefathers made of your natural advantages for commerce to their avarice, formed a deliberate plan to wrest from you the small pittance of property which they had permitted you to acquire. Remember that the men who wish to rule over you are they who, in pursuit of this plan of despotism, annulled the sacred contracts which had been made with your ancestors, conveyed into your cities a mercenary soldiery to compel you to submission by insult and murder, who called your patience cowardice, your piety hypocrisy.

Countrymen, the men who now invite you to surrender your rights into their hands are the men who have let loose the merciless savages to riot in the blood of their brethren, who have dared to establish popery triumphant in our land, who have taught treachery to your slaves, and courted them to assassinate your wives and children. These are the men to whom we are exhorted to sacrifice the blessings which Providence holds out to us - the happiness, the dignity, of uncontrolled freedom and independence.

Let not your generous indignation be directed against any among us who may advise so absurd and maddening a measure. Their number is but few, and daily decreases; and the spirit which can render them patient of slavery will render them contemptible enemies. Our union is now complete, our constitution composed, established, and approved. You are now the guardians of your own liberties. We may justly address you as the Decemviri did the Romans, and say,

Nothing that we propose can pass into a law without your consent. Be yourselves, O Americans, the authors of those laws on which your happiness depends.

You have now in the field armies sufficient to repel the whole force of your enemies and their base and mercenary auxiliaries. The hearts of your soldiers beat high with the spirit of freedom; they are animated with the justice of their cause, and, while they grasp their swords, can look up to Heaven for assistance. Your adversaries are composed of wretches who laugh at the rights of humanity, who turn religion into derision, and would, for higher wages, direct their swords against their leaders or their country. Go on, then, in your generous enterprise, with gratitude to Heaven for past success and confidence of it in the future. For my own part, I ask no greater blessing than to share with you the common danger and common glory. If I have a wish dearer to my soul than that my ashes may be mingled with those of a Warren and Montgomery, it is that these American states may never cease to be free and independent.

Afterward

His friends and admirers called Samuel *Adams The Man of the Revolution* and *The First Politician in the World.* His enemies and detractors called him *The Machiavelli of Chaos* and *The American Cromwell.* After signing the Declaration of Independence Samuel Adams went on to serve in the Continental Congress until 1781. In 1788, as a delegate to the Federal Constitutional Convention, he voted to ratify the United States Constitution. In Massachusetts he served as a delegate to the Massachusetts Constitutional Convention, President of the Massachusetts State Senate, Massachusetts Lieutenant Governor, and as Massachusetts Governor. Samuel Adams died on October 2, 1803 and is buried in Boston's Old Granary Cemetery.

Selected Reading

Cushing, Harry, *The Writings of Samuel Adams,* 1906.

Harlow, Ralph, *Samuel Adams: Promoter of the Revolution,* 1923.

Hosmer, James, *Samuel Adams,* 1885.

Miller, John, *Sam Adams: Pioneer in Propaganda,* 1936.

Wells, William, *The Life and Public Services of Samuel Adams,* 1865.

Mary Easty
A "Salem Witch" Pleads For Mercy
September 9, 1692

Death shall be assigned to any that shall employ evil spirits.

**- The Salem Witchcraft Law
(1629)**

Salem Village was founded in 1629 by *The People of God*, as the Puritans called themselves. One of the Puritan beliefs was that witchcraft, *cavorting with Satan*, was an act of rebellion against God. *The Salem Witch Hunt* began in 1692, when several of the Village's young women, *the Afflicted Girls*, began to report terrifying ghostly visions of witches who threatened their lives and tortured their souls. Two of those accused were the *the Towne Sisters*, Rebecca Nurse and Mary Easty.

William and Joanna (Blessing) Towne brought their family from England to Salem in 1634. Rebecca married Francis Nurse and raised eight children. Mary Towne married Isaac Easty and raised nine children. *Goody* Nurse and *Goody* Easty had lived in peace in Salem for over fifty years. Both were arrested on charges of witchcraft and imprisoned in Salem's *Witch Jail*, where they and others accused were kept chained to the walls, ill-fed, ill-clothed, and ill-treated. Four fellow prisoners died awaiting trial.

In preparation for the Witchcraft Trials, the judges (called *the Unmerciful Men*) enacted a civil death penalty statute. On June 10 the first convicted witch was hung. Rebecca's witchcraft trial was held on June 29, 1692. She was found guilty and, with four other *Salem Witches*, was executed on July 19. Mary's witchcraft trial was held on September 9, 1692. The jury found proof of her guilt in the hallucinations and hysterics of her accusers. The judges sentenced her to death. The *Condemned Witch Mary Easty* made the following moving plea to the Court.

Mary Easty

I, the poor and humble Mary Easty, being condemned to die, do humbly beg of you to take it in your judicious and pious consideration that your poor and humble petitioner, knowing my own innocency - blessed be the Lord for it! - and seeing plainly the wiles and subtlety of my accusers by myself, cannot but judge charitably of others that are going the same way of myself, if the Lord steps not mightily in. I was confined a whole month upon the same account that I am condemned now for, and then cleared by the afflicted persons, as some of Your Honors know. And in two days' time I was cried out upon them, and have been confined, and now am condemned to die. The Lord above knows my innocency then, and likewise does now, as at the great day will be known to men and angels.

I petition to Your Honors not for my own life, for I know I must die, and my appointed time is set; but the Lord he knows it is that, if it be possible, no more innocent blood may be shed, which undoubtedly cannot be avoided in the way and course you go in. I question not but Your Honors do to the utmost of your powers in the discovery and detecting of witchcraft and witches, and would not be guilty of innocent blood for the world. But, by my own innocency, I know you are in the wrong way. The Lord in his infinite mercy direct you in this great work, if it be his blessed will that no more innocent blood be shed! I would humbly beg of you that Your Honors would be pleased to examine these afflicted persons strictly, and keep them apart some time, and likewise to try some of these confessing witches, I being confident there is several of them has belied themselves and others, as will appear, if not in this world, I am sure in the world to come, whither I am now agoing.

Mary Easty

I question not but you will see an alteration of these things. They say myself and others having made a league with the Devil, we cannot confess. I know, and the Lord knows, as will . . . appear, they belie me, and so I question not but they do others. The Lord above, who is the Searcher of all hearts, knows, as I shall answer it at the tribunal seat, that I know not the least thing of witchcraft; therefore I cannot, I dare not, belie my own soul. I beg Your Honors not to deny this my humble petition from a poor, dying, innocent person. And I question not but the Lord will give a blessing to your endeavors.

Afterward

On September 22 Mary Easty was taken through the streets of Salem Village to Gallows Hill. *Her last farewell,* reported an eyewitness, *of her husband, children, and friends was as serious, religious, distinct, and affectionate as could well be expressed, drawing tears from the eyes of almost all present.* Along with seven other women, she was hanged. These were the last of the nineteen witchcraft executions in Salem, Massachusetts.

Selected Reading

Boyer, Paul, *Salem Possessed,* 1974.
Cahill, Robert, *Horrors of Salem's Witch Dungeon,* 1986.
Levin, David, *What Happened in Salem,* 1960.
Karlsen, Carol, *The Devil in the Shape of a Woman,* 1987.
Kittridge, George, *Witchcraft in Old New England,* 1920.
Nevins, Winfield, *Witchcraft in Salem Village,* 1961.
Robinson, Enders, *The Devil Discovered,* 1962.
Rosenthal, Bernard, *Salem Story,* 1993.
Starkey, Marion, *The Devil in Massachusetts,* 1949.
Thompson, Roger, *The Witches of Salem,* 1982.

Fiction
Miller, Arthur, *The Crucible,* 1984.

Jonathan Edwards
Sinners In The Hands Of An Angry God
July 8, 1741

His words often discovered a great degree of inward fervor and fell with great weight on the minds of his hearers.
- **The Life and Character of Jonathan Edwards (1765)**

In the early 1740's, the Great Awakening, an evangelical revival, swept like wildfire through the Christian faithful of colonial New England. Believing that the biblically prophesied end of the world was close at hand, pastors throughout New England began to preach terror-filled *damnation or salvation* sermons. Parishioners listening to these sermons were whipped into fits of *spiritual rapture.*

Reverend Jonathan Edwards became the leading voice of the *Hellfire Preachers.* Accounts say that in his sermons the Reverend Edwards *used no gestures, but stood motionless, with his eyes fixed straight in front of him. His voice low and distinct, going on pitilessly, like the voice of God Himself. His solemnity and sincerity so impressive, his descriptions of the fate of sinners so realistic, that his hearers were moved to agonies of tears and supplications.*

Jonathan Edwards, son, grandson, and great-grandson of clergymen, was born on October 5, 1703 in East Windsor, Connecticut to the Reverend Timothy Edwards and Ester (Stoddard) Edwards. Educated in theology at Yale, he became in 1726 assistant to and then in 1729 successor to his grandfather's pulpit in Northampton, Massachusetts.

Already famous throughout New England for delivering two great *Hellfire* sermons - *Eternity In Hell* and *The Wrath Of God* - the Reverend Jonathan Edwards was invited to preach to a congregation in the rural village of Enfield, Connecticut. There, on July 8, 1741, he delivered the Great Awakening's most famous *damnation or salvation* sermon, *Sinners In The Hands Of An Angry God.*

Vengeance is mine, and recompense, against the time when their foot shall slip, for the day of their calamity is at hand, and their doom comes swiftly. In this verse (Deuteronomy 32:35) is threatened the vengeance of God on the wicked, unbelieving Israelites, who were God's visible people, and who lived under the means of grace, but who, notwithstanding all God's wonderful works towards them, remained void of counsel, having no understanding in them. Under all the cultivations of heaven, they brought forth bitter and poisonous fruit. The expression I have chosen for my text, *Their foot shall slide in due time*, seems to imply the following things, relating to the punishment and destruction to which these wicked Israelites were exposed.

That they were always exposed to destruction, as one that stands or walks in slippery places is always exposed to fall. This is implied in the manner of their destruction coming upon them, being represented by their foot sliding. The same is expressed, *Surely thou didst set them in slippery places; thou castedst them down into destruction.*

It implies that they were always exposed to sudden unexpected destruction. As he that walks in slippery places is every moment liable to fall, he cannot foresee one moment whether he shall stand or fall the next; and when he does fall, he falls at once without warning. *Surely thou didst set them in slippery places; thou castedst them down into destruction; how are they brought into desolation as in a moment!*

Another thing implied is that they are liable to fall of themselves, without being thrown down by the hand of another, as he that stands or walks on slippery ground needs nothing but his own weight to throw him down.

That the reason why they are not fallen already, and do not fall now, is only that God's appointed time is not come. For it is said, that when that due time, or appointed time, comes, their foot shall slide. Then they shall be left to fall, as they are inclined by their own weight. God will not hold them up in these slippery places any longer, but will let them go; and then, at that very instant, they shall fall into destruction; as he that stands on such slippery declining ground, on the edge of a pit, he cannot stand alone; when he is let go he immediately falls and is lost.

The observation from the words that I would now insist upon is this - *There is nothing that keeps wicked men at any one moment out of hell, but the mere pleasure of God.* By the mere pleasure of God I mean his sovereign pleasure, his arbitrary will, restrained by no obligation, hindered by no manner of difficulty, any more than if nothing else but God's mere will had in the least degree, or in any respect whatsoever, any hand in the preservation of wicked men one moment. The truth of this observation may appear by the following considerations.

There is no want of power in God to cast wicked men into hell at any moment. Men's hands cannot be strong when God rises up. The strongest have no power to resist him, nor can any deliver out of his hands. He is not only able to cast wicked men into hell, but he can most easily do it. Sometimes an earthly prince meets with a great deal of difficulty to subdue a rebel, who has found means to fortify himself, and has made himself strong by the numbers of his followers. But it is not so with God. There is no fortress that is any defense from the power of God. Though hand join in hand, and vast multitudes of God's enemies combine and associate themselves, they are easily broken in pieces. They are as great heaps of light chaff before the whirlwind, or large quantities of dry stubble before devouring flames. We find it easy to tread on and crush a worm that we see crawling on the earth; so it is easy for us to cut or singe a slender thread that any thing hangs by - thus easy is it for God, when he pleases, to cast his enemies down to hell. What are we, that we should think to stand before him, at whose rebuke the earth trembles, and before whom the rocks are thrown down?

They deserve to be cast into hell, so that divine justice never stands in the way; it makes no objection against God's using his power at any moment to destroy them. Yea, on the contrary, justice calls aloud for an infinite punishment of their sins. Divine justice says of the tree that brings forth such grapes of Sodom, *Cut it down, why cumbereth it the ground?* The sword of divine justice is every moment brandished over their heads, and it is nothing but the hand of arbitrary mercy, and God's mere will, that holds it back.

They are already under a sentence of condemnation to hell. They do not only justly deserve to be cast down thither, but the sentence of the law of God, that eternal and immutable rule of righteousness that God has fixed between him and mankind, is gone out against them, and stands against them, so that they are bound over already to hell. *He that believeth not is condemned already.* So that every unconverted man properly belongs to hell; that is his place; from thence he is. *Ye are from beneath.* And thither he is bound; it is the place that justice, and God's word, and the sentence of his unchangeable law assign to him.

They are now the objects of that very same anger and wrath of God that is expressed in the torments of hell. And the reason why they do not go down to hell at each moment is not because God, in whose power they are, is not then very angry with them, as he is with many miserable creatures now tormented in hell, who there feel and bear the fierceness of his wrath. Yea, God is a great deal more angry with great numbers that are now on earth - yea, doubtless, with many that are now in this congregation, who it may be are at ease - than he is with many of those who are now in the flames of hell.

So that it is not because God is unmindful of their wickedness, and does not resent it, that he does not let loose his hand and cut them off. God is not altogether such a one as themselves, though they may imagine him to be so. The wrath of God burns against them, their damnation does not slumber; the pit is prepared, the fire is made ready, the furnace is now hot, ready to receive them; the flames do now rage and glow. The glittering sword is whet, and held over them, and the pit hath opened its mouth under them.

The devil stands ready to fall upon them, and seize them as his own, at what moment God shall permit him. They belong to him; he has their souls in his possession, and under his dominion. The scripture represents them as his goods. The devils watch them; they are ever by them at their right hand; they stand waiting for them, like greedy hungry lions that see their prey, and expect to have it, but are for the present kept back. If God should withdraw his hand, by which they are restrained, they would in one moment fly upon their poor souls. The old serpent is gaping for them; hell opens its mouth wide to receive them, and, if God should permit it, they would be hastily swallowed up and lost.

There are in the souls of wicked men those hellish principles reigning, that would presently kindle and flame out into hell fire, if it were not for God's restraints. There is laid in the very nature of carnal men a foundation for the torments of hell. There are those corrupt principles, in reigning power in them, and in full possession of them, that are seeds of hell fire. These principles are active and powerful, exceeding violent in their nature, and if it were not for the restraining hand of God upon them, they would soon break out; they would flame out after the same manner as the same corruptions, the same enmity does in the hearts of damned souls, and would beget the same torments as they do in them. . . .

It is no security to wicked men for one moment that there are no visible means of death at hand. It is no security to a natural man, that he is now in health, and that he does not see which way he should now immediately go out of the world by an accident, and that there is no visible danger in any respect in his circumstances. The manifold and continual experience of the world in all ages shows this is no evidence, that a man is not on the very brink of eternity, and that the next step will not be into another world. The unseen, unthought-of ways and means of persons going suddenly out of the world are innumerable and inconceivable. Unconverted men walk over the pit of hell on a rotten covering, and there are innumerable places in this covering so weak that they will not bear their weight, and these places are not seen. The arrows of death fly unseen at noon-day; the sharpest sight cannot discern them. God has so many different unsearchable ways of taking wicked men out of the world and sending them to hell that there is nothing to make it appear that God has need to be at the expense of a miracle, or go out of the ordinary course of his providence, to destroy any wicked man, at any moment. All the means that there are of sinners going out of the world are so in God's hands, and so universally and absolutely subject to his power and determination, that it does not depend at all the less on the mere will of God whether sinners shall at any moment go to hell, than if means were never made use of, or at all concerned in the case.

Natural men's prudence and care to preserve their own lives, or the care of others to preserve them, do not secure them a moment. To this, divine providence and universal experience do also bear testimony. . . . *How dieth the wise man? even as the fool.*

All wicked men's pains and contrivance which they use to escape hell, while they continue to reject Christ, and so remain wicked men, do not secure them from hell one moment. Almost every natural man that hears of hell flatters himself that he shall escape it; he depends upon himself for his own security; he flatters himself in what he has done, in what he is now doing, or what he intends to do. Every one lays out matters in his own mind how he shall avoid damnation, and flatters himself that he contrives well for himself, and that his schemes will not fail. They hear indeed that there are but few saved, and that the greater part of men that have died heretofore are gone to hell; but each one imagines that he lays out matters better for his own escape than others have done. He does not intend to come to that place of torment; he says within himself that he intends to take effectual care, and to order matters so for himself as not to fail.

But the foolish children of men miserably delude themselves in their own schemes, and in confidence in their own strength and wisdom; they trust to nothing but a shadow. The greater part of those who heretofore have lived under the same means of grace, and are now dead, are undoubtedly gone to hell; and it was not because they were not as wise as those who are now alive; it was not because they did not lay out matters as well for themselves to secure their own escape. If we could speak with them, and inquire of them, one by one, whether they expected, when alive, and when they used to hear about hell, ever to be the subjects of that misery, we doubtless should hear one and another reply,

No, I never intended to come here. I had laid out matters otherwise in my mind. I thought I should contrive well for myself; I thought my scheme good. I intended to take effectual care; but it came upon me unexpected; I did not look for it at that time, and in that manner; it came as a thief. Death outwitted me - God's wrath was too quick for me. Oh, my cursed foolishness! I was flattering myself, and pleasing myself with vain dreams of what I would do hereafter; and when I was saying, Peace and safety, then suddenly destruction came upon me.

God has laid himself under no obligation, by any promise to keep any natural man out of hell one moment. God certainly has made no promises either of eternal life, or of any deliverance or preservation from eternal death, but what are contained in the covenant of grace, the promises that are given in Christ, in whom all the promises are yea and amen. But surely they have no interest in the promises of the covenant of grace who are not the children of the covenant, who do not believe in any of the promises, and have no interest in the Mediator of the covenant. So that, whatever some have imagined and pretended about promises made to natural men's earnest seeking and knocking, it is plain and manifest that whatever pains a natural man takes in religion, whatever prayers he makes, till he believes in Christ, God is under no manner of obligation to keep him a moment from eternal destruction.

. . . . The use of this awful subject may be for awakening unconverted persons in this congregation. This that you have heard is the case of every one of you that are out of Christ. That world of misery, that lake of burning brimstone, is extended abroad under you. There is the dreadful pit of the glowing flames of the wrath of God; there is hell's wide gaping mouth open; and you have nothing to stand upon, nor any thing to take hold of. There is nothing between you and hell but the air; it is only the power and mere pleasure of God that holds you up.

You probably are not sensible of this; you find you are kept out of hell, but do not see the hand of God in it. But look at other things, as the good state of your bodily constitution, your care of your own life, and the means you use for your own preservation. But indeed these things are nothing; if God should withdraw his hand, they would avail no more to keep you from falling than the thin air to hold up a person that is suspended in it.

Your wickedness makes you as it were heavy as lead, and to tend downwards with great weight and pressure towards hell; and if God should let you go, you would immediately sink and swiftly descend and plunge into the bottomless gulf, and your healthy constitution, and your own care and prudence, and best contrivance, and all your righteousness, would have no more influence to uphold you and keep you out of hell than a spider's web would have to stop a fallen rock. Were it not for the sovereign pleasure of God, the earth would not bear you one moment, for you are a burden to it. The creation groans with you; the creature is made subject to the bondage of your corruption, not willingly. The sun does not willingly shine upon you to give you light to serve sin and Satan; the earth does not willingly yield her increase to satisfy your lusts, nor is it willingly a stage for your wickedness to be acted upon; the air does not willingly serve you for breath to maintain the flame of life in your vitals, while you spend your life in the service of God's enemies. God's creatures are good, and were made for men to serve God with, and do not willingly subserve to any other purpose, and groan when they are abused to purposes so directly contrary to their nature and end. And the world would spew you out, were it not for the sovereign hand of him who hath subjected it in hope. There are black clouds of God's wrath now hanging directly over your heads, full of the dreadful storm, and big with thunder, and were it not for the restraining hand of God, it would immediately burst forth upon you. The sovereign pleasure of God, for the present, stays his rough wind; otherwise it would come with fury, and your destruction would come like a whirlwind, and you would be like the chaff of the summer threshing floor.

. . . . The bow of God's wrath is bent, and the arrow made ready on the string, and justice bends the arrow at your heart, and strains the bow, and it is nothing but the mere pleasure of God, and that of an angry God, without any promise or obligation at all, that keeps the arrow one moment from being made drunk with your blood. Thus all you that never passed under a great change of heart, by the mighty power of the Spirit of God upon your souls, all you that were never born again, and made new creatures, and raised from being dead in sin to a state of new, and before altogether unexperienced light and life, are in the hands of an angry God. However you may have reformed your life in many things, and may have had religious affections, and may keep up a form of religion in your families and closets, and in the house of God, it is nothing but his mere pleasure that keeps you from being this moment swallowed up in everlasting destruction. . . .

The God that holds you over the pit of hell, much as one holds a spider or some loathsome insect over the fire, abhors you, and is dreadfully provoked. His wrath towards you burns like fire; he looks upon you as worthy of nothing else but to be cast into the fire. He is of purer eyes than to bear to have you in his sight; you are ten thousand times more abominable in his eyes than the most hateful venomous serpent is in ours. You have offended him infinitely more than ever a stubborn rebel did his prince; and yet it is nothing but his hand that holds you from falling into the fire every moment. It is to be ascribed to nothing else that you did not go to hell the last night; that you was suffered to awake again in this world, after you closed your eyes to sleep. And there is no other reason to be given why you have not dropped into hell since you arose in the morning, but that God's hand has held you up. There is no other reason to be given why you have not gone to hell, since you have sat here in the house of God, provoking his pure eyes by your sinful wicked manner of attending his solemn worship. Yea, there is nothing else that is to be given as a reason why you do not this very moment drop down into hell.

Oh sinner! Consider the fearful danger you are in - it is a great furnace of wrath, a wide and bottomless pit, full of the fire of wrath, that you are held over in the hand of that God, whose wrath is provoked and incensed as much against you as against many of the damned in hell. You hang by a slender thread, with the flames of divine wrath flashing about it, and ready every moment to singe it, and burn it asunder; and you have no interest in any Mediator, and nothing to lay hold of to save yourself, nothing to keep off the flames of wrath, nothing of your own, nothing that you ever have done, nothing that you can do, to induce God to spare you one moment. And consider here more particularly whose wrath it is - it is the wrath of the infinite God. If it were only the wrath of man, though it were of the most potent prince, it would be comparatively little to be regarded. The wrath of kings is very much dreaded, especially of absolute monarchs, who have the possessions and lives of their subjects wholly in their power, to be disposed of at their mere will. *The fear of a king is as the roaring of a lion - Whoso provoketh him to anger sinneth against his own soul.* . . . All the kings of the earth, before God, are as grasshoppers; they are nothing, and less than nothing - both their love and their hatred is to be despised. The wrath of the great King of kings is as much more terrible than theirs as his majesty is greater.

And I say unto you, my friends - Be not afraid of them that kill the body, and after that, have no more that they can do. But I will forewarn you whom you shall fear - fear him which, after he hath killed, hath power to cast into hell - yea, I say unto you, fear him.

It is the fierceness of his wrath that you are exposed to. We often read of the fury of God,

According to their deeds, accordingly he will repay fury to his adversaries. . . . *For behold, the Lord will come with fire and with his chariots like a whirlwind, to render his anger with fury, and his rebuke with flames of fire.*

And . . . we read of *the wine press of the fierceness and wrath of Almighty God.* The words are exceeding terrible. If it had only been said, *the wrath of God,* the words would have implied that which is infinitely dreadful; but it is *the fierceness and wrath of God.* The fury of God! the fierceness of Jehovah! Oh, how dreadful must that be! Who can utter or conceive what such expressions carry in them! But it is also *the fierceness and wrath of Almighty God,* as though there would be a very great manifestation of his almighty power in what the fierceness of his wrath should inflict, as though omnipotence should be as it were enraged, and exerted, as men are wont to exert their strength in the fierceness of their wrath. Oh! then, what will be the consequence! What will become of the poor worms that shall suffer it! Whose hands can be strong? And whose heart can endure? To what a dreadful, inexpressible, inconceivable depth of misery must the poor creature be sunk who shall be the subject of this!

Consider this, you that are here present, that yet remain in an unregenerate state. That God will execute the fierceness of his anger implies that he will inflict wrath without any pity. When God beholds the ineffable extremity of your case, and sees your torment to be so vastly disproportioned to your strength, and sees how your poor soul is crushed, and sinks down, as it were, into an infinite gloom, he will have no compassion upon you. He will not forbear the executions of his wrath, or in the least lighten his hand; there shall be no moderation or mercy, nor will God then at all stay his rough wind; he will have no regard to your welfare, nor be at all careful lest you should suffer too much in any other sense, than only that you shall not suffer beyond what strict justice requires. Nothing shall be withheld, because it is so hard for you to bear. *Therefore will I also deal in fury; mine eye shall not spare, neither will I have pity; and though they cry in mine ears with a loud voice, yet I will not hear them.* Now God stands ready to pity you; this is a day of mercy; you may cry now with some encouragement of obtaining mercy. But when once the day of mercy is past, your most lamentable and dolorous cries and shrieks will be in vain; you will be wholly lost and thrown away of God, as to any regard to your welfare. God will have no other use to put you to but to suffer misery; you shall be continued in being to no other end, for you will be a vessel of wrath fitted to destruction, and there will be no other use of this vessel, but to be filled full of wrath. God will be so far from pitying you when you cry to him that it is said he will only *laugh and mock.*

How awful are those words, which are the words of the great God. *I will tread them in mine anger, and will trample them in my fury, and their blood shall be sprinkled upon my garments, and I will stain all my raiment.* It is perhaps impossible to conceive of words that carry in them greater manifestations of these three things - contempt, and hatred, and fierceness of indignation. If you cry to God to pity you, he will be so far from pitying you in your doleful case, or showing you the least regard or favor, that instead of that, he will only tread you under foot. And though he will know that you cannot bear the weight of omnipotence treading upon you, yet he will not regard that, but he will crush you under his feet without mercy; he will crush out your blood, and make it fly, and it shall be sprinkled on his garments, so as to stain all his raiment. He will not only hate you, but he will have you in the utmost contempt - no place shall be thought fit for you but under his feet to be trodden down as the mire of the streets.

The misery you are exposed to is that which God will inflict to that end, that he might show what that wrath of Jehovah is. God hath had it on his heart to show to angels and men both how excellent his love is, and also how terrible his wrath is. Sometimes earthly kings have a mind to show how terrible their wrath is, by the extreme punishments they would excute on those that would provoke them. Nebuchadnezzar, that mighty and haughty monarch of the Chaldean empire, was willing to show his wrath when enraged with Shadrach, Meshech, and Abednego, and accordingly gave orders that the burning fiery furnace should be heated seven times hotter than it was before; doubtless, it was raised to the utmost degree of fierceness that human art could raise it. But the great God is also willing to show his wrath and magnify his awful majesty and mighty power in the extreme sufferings of his enemies. *What if God, willing to show his wrath, and to make his power known, endure with much long-suffering the vessels of wrath fitted to destruction?* And seeing this is his design, and what he has determined, even to show how terrible the unrestrained wrath, the fury and fierceness of Jehovah is, he will do it to effect. There will be something accomplished and brought to pass that will be dreadful with a witness. When the great and angry God hath risen up and executed his awful vengeance on the poor sinner, and the wretch is actually suffering the infinite weight and power of his indignation, then will God call upon the whole universe to behold that awful majesty and mighty power that is to be seen in it.

And the people shall be as the burnings of lime, as thorns cut up shall they be burnt in the fire. Hear ye that are far off, what I have done; and ye that are near, acknowledge my might. The sinners in Zion are afraid; fearfulness hath surprised the hypocrites.

Thus it will be with you that are in an unconverted state, if you continue in it; the infinite might, and majesty, and terribleness of the omnipotent God shall be magnified upon you, in the ineffable strength of your torments. You shall be tormented in the presence of the holy angels, and in the presence of the Lamb; and when you shall be in this state of suffering, the glorious inhabitants of heaven shall go forth and look on the awful spectacle, that they may see what the wrath and fierceness of the Almighty is; and when they have seen it, they will fall down and adore that great power and majesty.

And it shall come to pass, that from one new moon to another, and from one Sabbath to another, shall all flesh come to worship before me, saith the Lord. And they shall go forth and look upon the carcasses of the men that have transgressed against me, for their worm shall not die; neither shall their fire be quenched, and they shall be an abhorring unto all flesh.

It is everlasting wrath. It would be dreadful to suffer this fierceness and wrath of Almighty God one moment, but you must suffer it to all eternity. There will be no end to this exquisite horrible misery. When you look forward, you shall see a long forever, a boundless duration before you, which will swallow up your thoughts, and amaze your soul; and you will absolutely despair of ever having any deliverance, any end, any mitigation, any rest at all. You will know certainly that you must wear out long ages, millions of millions of ages, in wrestling and conflicting with this almighty merciless vengeance; and then when you have so done, when so many ages have actually been spent by you in this manner, you will know that all is but a point to what remains. So that your punishment will indeed be infinite. Oh, who can express what the state of a soul in such circumstances is! All that we can possibly say about it gives but a very feeble, faint representation of it; it is inexpressible and inconceivable, for *who knows the power of God's anger?*

How dreadful is the state of those that are daily and hourly in the danger of this great wrath and infinite misery! But this is the dismal case of every soul in this congregation that has not been born again, however moral and strict, sober and religious, they may otherwise be. Oh, that you would consider it, whether you be young or old! There is reason to think that there are many in this congregation now hearing this discourse that will actually be the subjects of this very misery to all eternity. We know not who they are, or in what seats they sit, or what thoughts they now have. It may be they are now at ease, and hear all these things without much disturbance, and are now flattering themselves that they are not the persons, promising themselves that they shall escape. If we knew that there was one person, and but one, in the whole congregation, that was to be the subject of this misery, what an awful thing would it be to think of! If we knew who it was, what an awful sight would it be to see such a person! How might all the rest of the congregation lift up a lamentable and bitter cry over him! But, alas! instead of one, how many is it likely will remember this discourse in hell? And it would be a wonder if some that are now present should not be in hell in a very short time, even before this year is out. And it would be no wonder if some persons that now sit here, in some seats of this meeting-house, in health, quiet and secure, should be there before tomorrow morning. Those of you that finally continue in a natural condition, that shall keep out of hell longest, will be there in a little time! Your damnation does not slumber; it will come swiftly, and, in all probability, very suddenly upon many of you - you have reason to wonder that you are not already in hell. It is doubtless the case of some whom you have seen and known, that never deserved hell more than you, and that heretofore appeared as likely to have been now alive as you. Their case is past all hope; they are crying in extreme misery and perfect despair; but here you are in the land of the living and in the house of God, and have an opportunity to obtain salvation. What would not those poor damned hopeless souls give for one day's opportunity such as you now enjoy!

And now you have an extraordinary opportunity, a day wherein Christ has thrown the door of mercy wide open, and stands in calling and crying with a loud voice to poor sinners - a day wherein many are flocking to him, and pressing into the kingdom of God. Many are daily coming from the east, west, north, and south; many that were very lately in the same miserable condition that you are in are now in a happy state, with their hearts filled with love to him who has loved them, and washed them from their sins in his own blood, and rejoicing in hope of the glory of

God. How awful is it to be left behind at such a day! To see so many others feasting, while you are pining and perishing! To see so many rejoicing and singing for joy of heart, while you have cause to mourn for sorrow of heart, and howl for vexation of spirit! How can you rest one moment in such a condition? Are not your souls as precious as the souls of the people at Suffield, where they are flocking from day to day to Christ?

Are there not many here who have lived long in the world and are not to this day born again? And so are aliens from the commonwealth of Israel, and have done nothing ever since they have lived, but treasure up wrath against the day of wrath? Oh, sirs, your case, in an especial manner, is extremely dangerous. Your guilt and hardness of heart is extremely great. Do you not see how generally persons of your years are passed over and left, in the present remarkable and wonderful dispensation of God's mercy? You had need to consider yourselves, and awake thoroughly out of sleep. You cannot bear the fierceness and wrath of the infinite God. And you, young men, and young women, will you neglect this precious season which you now enjoy, when so many others of your age are renouncing all youthful vanities and flocking to Christ? You especially have now an extraordinary opportunity; but if you neglect it, it will soon be with you as with those persons who spent all the precious days of youth in sin, and are now come to such a dreadful pass in blindness and hardness. And you, children, who are unconverted, do not you know that you are going down to hell, to bear the dreadful wrath of that God, who is now angry with you every day and every night? Will you be content to be the children of the devil, when so many other children in the land are converted, and are become the holy and happy children of the King of kings?

And let every one that is yet of Christ, and hanging over the pit of hell, whether they be old men and women, or middle aged, or young people, or little children, now hearken to the loud calls of God's word and providence. This acceptable year of the Lord, a day of such great favors to some, will doubtless be a day of as remarkable vengeance to others. Men's hearts harden, and their guilt increases apace at such a day as this, if they neglect their souls; and never was there so great danger of such persons being given up to hardness of heart and blindness of mind. God seems now to be hastily gathering in his elect in all parts of the land; and probably the greater part of adult persons that ever shall be saved will be brought in now in a little time, and it will be as it was on the great out-pouring of the Spirit upon the Jews in the apostles' days - the election will obtain, and the rest will be blinded. If this should be the case with you, you will eternally curse this day, and will curse the day that ever you was born, to see such a season of the pouring out of God's Spirit, and will wish that you had died and gone to hell before you had seen it. Now undoubtedly it is, as it was in the days of John the Baptist, the axe is in an extraordinary manner laid at the root of the trees, that every tree which brings not forth good fruit may be hewn down and cast into the fire.

Therefore, let every one that is out of Christ now awake and fly from the wrath to come. The wrath of Almighty God is now undoubtedly hanging over a great part of this congregation. Let every one fly out of Sodom - *Haste and escape for your lives, look not behind you, escape to the mountain, lest you be consumed.*

Jonathan Edwards

Afterward

The Great Awakening: After reaching its high water mark in 1744, New England's religious revival, *the Great Awakening,* began to wane in general popularity. The clergy, including Jonathan Edwards, who had at first embraced *damnation or salvation,* began to back off as lay splinter groups, criticized for being overly excessive, broke off from the established churches, denouncing the clergy *as hirelings of Satan leading their flocks to Hell.* These splinter groups continued their own *hellfire revivals,* sparking flare-ups, the largest occurring in the South beginning in 1748, before dying out.

Jonathan Edwards: Drawing from his personal observations of the successes and excesses of *the Great Awakening,* Edwards wrote *Thoughts Concerning the Present Revival in New England* (1742) and *A Treatise Concerning Religious Affections* (1746). In 1750, in a bitter doctrinal dispute, he was relieved after a twenty-year tenure of his position as Minister to the Northampton Congregation. He continued to be a writer - *The Great Christian Doctrine of Original Sin Defended* (1758), a minister - to a Stockbridge church, a missionary - to an Indian school, and a teacher -   President of Princeton College. He died on March 22, 1758.

Selected Reading

Allen, Alexander V.G., *Jonathan Edwards,* 1891.

Heimert, Alan, *Religion and the American Mind, From the Great Awakening to the Revolution,* 1966.

Hopkind, Samuel, *The Life and Character of Reverend Jonathan Edwards,* 1765.

Levin, David, *Jonathan Edwards: A Profile,* 1969.

Parkes, Henry, *Jonathan Edwards: The Fiery Puritan,* 1930.

Winslow, Ola E., *Jonathan Edwards, 1703-1758,* 1961.

Benjamin Franklin
The Signing Of The Constitution
September 17, 1787

My little speech. - **Benjamin Franklin (1787)**

Benjamin Franklin, born on January 17, 1706 in Boston, Massachusetts, the son of Josiah and Abiah (Folger) Franklin, led one of the most accomplished of all American lives. As a writer and publisher, he created *Poor Richard's Almanac.* As an early revolutionary, he told the Pennsylvania Assembly in 1755, *Those who would give up essential liberty to obtain a little temporary safety deserve neither liberty nor safety.* As a patriot, he helped draft and then signed the Declaration of Independence. As a scientist and inventor, he experimented with lightning and electricity. As a diplomat, he represented the United States at the Court of France. As a statesman, he negotiated an end to the Revolutionary War. As an educator and philosopher, he was the founder of both the University of Pennsylvania and the American Philosophical Society. As a public servant and politician, he served as the U.S. Postmaster General and the President of Pennsylvania.

Benjamin Franklin had been working for a permanent union of first the thirteen Colonies and then the thirteen States for more than thirty-three years when a Constitutional Convention was called in 1787. Meeting in Philadelphia, the job of the delegates was to reach a consensus for a permanent union among the thirteen states. Several Plans of Union were offered and debated before the Connecticut Compromise was reached and a draft Constitution was prepared. A vote, of which the outcome was uncertain, was scheduled for September 17, 1787.

Benjamin Franklin, at eight-two the oldest delegate to the Convention, was the last speaker scheduled before the final vote. Franklin, in poor health, sat silently by as fellow Pennsylvania delegate James Wilson read this landmark speech.

Mr. President, I confess that there are several parts of this Constitution which I do not at present approve, but I am not sure I shall never approve them, for, having lived long, I have experienced many instances of being obliged, by better information or fuller consideration, to change opinions even on important subjects which I once thought right but found to be otherwise.

It is therefore that the older I grow, the more apt I am to doubt my own judgment, and to pay more respect to the judgment of others. Most men indeed, as well as most sects in religion, think themselves in possession of all truth, and that whatever others differ from them it is so far error. Steele, a Protestant, in a dedication tells the Pope that the only difference between our churches in their opinions of the certainty of their doctrines is, the Church of Rome is infallible, and the Church of England is never in the wrong. But though many private persons think almost as highly of their own infallibility as of that of their sect, few express it so naturally as a certain French lady who, in a dispute with her sister, said, *I don't know how it happens, Sister, but I meet with nobody but myself that is always in the right.*

In these sentiments, Sir, I agree to this Constitution, with all its faults, if they are such, because I think a general government necessary for us, and there is no form of government but what may be a blessing to the people if well administered. And I believe farther that this is likely to be well administered for a course of years, and can only end in despotism, as other forms have done before it, when the people shall become so corrupted as to need despotic government, being incapable of any other. I doubt too whether any other Convention we can obtain may be able to make a better Constitution. For when you assemble a number of men to have the advantage of their joint wisdom, you inevitably assemble with those men all their prejudices, their passions, their errors of opinion, their local interests, and their selfish views. From such an assembly can a perfect production be expected? It therefore astonishes me, Sir, to find this system approaching so near to perfection as it does; and I think it will astonish our enemies, who are waiting with confidence to hear that our counsels are confounded like those of the builders of Babel, and that our States are on the point of separation, only to meet hereafter for the purpose of cutting one another's throats.

Thus I consent, Sir, to this Constitution, because I expect no better, and because I am not sure that it is not the best. The opinions I have had of its errors I sacrifice to the public good. I have never whispered a syllable of them abroad. Within these walls they were born, and here they shall die. If every one of us, in returning to our constituents, were to report the objections he has had to it, and endeavor to gain partisans in support of them, we might prevent its being generally received, and thereby lose all the salutary effects and great advantages resulting naturally in our favor among foreign nations, as well as among ourselves, from our real or apparent unanimity. Much of the strength and efficiency of any government in procuring and securing happiness to the people, depends on opinion, on the general opinion, of the goodness of the government, as well as of the wisdom and integrity of its governors. I hope therefore that for our own sakes, as a part of the people, and for the sake of our posterity, we shall act heartily and unanimously in recommending this Constitution, wherever our influence may extend, and turn our future thoughts and endeavors to the means of having it well administered.

On the whole, Sir, I cannot help expressing a wish that every member of the Convention who may still have objections to it would, with me on this occasion, doubt a little of his own infallibility, and, to make manifest our unanimity, put his name to this instrument.

Afterward

After Franklin's speech, the Constitution was approved by thirty-nine delegates and sent to the States for ratification. James Madison wrote in his *Journal, Whilst the last members were signing the Constitution, Doctor Franklin, looking towards the President's chair, at the back of which a sun happened to be painted, observed to a few members near him that painters had found it difficult to distinguish in their art a rising sun from a setting sun. "I have,"* said he, *"often and often, in the course of the session and vicissitudes of my hopes and fears as to its issue, looked at that behind the President, without being able to tell whether it was rising or setting, but now at length I have the happiness to know that it is a rising and not a setting sun."*

Benjamin Franklin died on April 17, 1790. Franklin's own epitaph reads, *The Body of Benjamin Franklin, Printer, (Like the cover of an old book, its contents torn out and stript of its lettering and gilding) Lies here, food for worms. But the work shall not be lost for it will (as he believed) appear once more, In a new and more elegant edition revised and corrected by The Author.*

Selected Reading

Aldridge, Alfred O., *Benjamin Franklin, Philosopher & Man*, 1965.

Cohen, I. Bernard, *Benjamin Franklin, Scientist and Statesman*, 1975.

Lopez, Claude Anne, and Eugenia W. Herbert, *The Private Franklin: The Man and His Family*, 1975.

Schoenbrun, David, *Triumph in Paris: The Exploits of Benjamin Franklin*, 1976.

Van Doren, Carl, *Benjamin Franklin*, 1938.

Alexander Hamilton
Republican Government
June 24, 1788

I trust the friends of the proposed Constitution will never concur with its enemies in questioning that fundamental principle of a republican government which admits the right of the people to alter or abolish the established Constitution whenever they find it inconsistent with their happiness.

- Alexander Hamilton, *The Federalist No. 78*

Alexander Hamilton was born on January 11, 1757 on Nevis, an island in the British West Indies, the son of James and Rachel (Faucette) Hamilton. He left his studies at Kings College (now Columbia University) to become involved with the revolutionary movement. At seventeen, Hamilton authored two pro-revolutionary political pamphlets - *A Full Vindication of the Measures of Congress for the Calumnies of Their Enemies* and *A More Comprehensive and Impartial View of the Disputes Between Great Britain and the Colonies.* These won him a widespread reputation. At the beginning of the Revolutionary War, Hamilton was given a military commission as a Lieutenant-Colonel and placed on the staff of General George Washington.

In 1782-1783 Hamilton represented New York in the Continental Congress. In 1786 he called for a Constitutional Convention. Hamilton, the only representative from New York, signed the Constitution for his State and returned to New York to work for its ratification. Along with James Madison and John Jay, he published *The Federalist Papers* - eighty-five political essays outlining reasons why the ratification of the Constitution was vital to the United States.

At New York State's Ratification Convention, the first day's unofficial vote count showed a majority against ratification. Hamilton worked tirelessly to turn the vote in his favor. On June 24 he delivered this landmark speech.

I am persuaded, Mr. Chairman, that I in my turn shall be indulged in addressing the committee. We all, in equal sincerity, profess to be anxious for the establishment of a republican government, on a safe and solid basis. It is the object of the wishes of every honest man in the United States, and I presume that I shall not be disbelieved, when I declare that it is an object of all others the nearest and most dear to my own heart. The means of accomplishing this great purpose become the most important study which can interest mankind. It is our duty to examine all those means with peculiar attention, and to choose the best and most effectual. It is our duty to draw from nature, from reason, from examples, the best principles of policy, and to pursue and apply them in the formation of our government. We should contemplate and compare the systems which, in this examination, come under our view; distinguish, with a careful eye, the defects and excellencies of each; and, discarding the former, incorporate the latter, as far as circumstances will admit, into our Constitution. If we pursue a different course and neglect this duty, we shall probably disappoint the expectations of our country and of the world.

In the commencement of a revolution, which received its birth from the usurpations of tyranny, nothing was more natural than that the public mind should be influenced by an extreme spirit of jealousy. To resist these encroachments and to nourish this spirit was the great object of all our public and private institutions. The zeal for liberty became predominant and excessive. In forming our Confederation, this passion alone seemed to actuate us, and we appear to have had no other view than to secure ourselves from despotism. The object certainly was a valuable one, and deserved our utmost attention. But, sir, there is another object equally important, and which our enthusiasm rendered us little capable of regarding. I mean a principle of strength and stability in the organization of our government, and vigor in its operations. This purpose can never be accomplished but by the establishment of some select body, formed peculiarly upon this principle. There are few positions more demonstrable than that there should be in every republic some permanent body to correct the prejudices, check the intemperate passions, and regulate the fluctuations of a popular assembly. It is evident that a body instituted for these purposes must be so formed as to exclude as much as possible from its own character those infirmities and that mutability which it is designed to remedy. It is therefore necessary that it should be small, that it should hold its authority during a considerable period, and that it should have such an independence in the exercise of its powers as will divest it as much as possible of local prejudices. It should be so formed as to be the center of political knowledge, to pursue always a steady line of conduct, and to reduce every irregular propensity to system. Without this establishment, we may make experiments without end, but shall never have an efficient government.

It is an unquestionable truth that the body of the people in every country desire sincerely its prosperity; but it is equally unquestionable, that they do not possess the discernment and stability necessary for systematic government. To deny that they are frequently led into the grossest errors by misinformation and passion would be a flattery which their own good sense must despise. That branch of administration especially which involves our political relations with foreign States a community will ever be incompetent to. These truths are not often held up in public assemblies, but they cannot be unknown to any who hear me. From these principles it follows that there ought to be two distinct bodies in our government - one which shall be immediately constituted by and peculiarly represent the people, and possess all the popular features; another formed upon the principle and for the purposes before explained. Such considerations as these induced the Convention who formed your State Constitution, to institute a Senate upon the present plan. The history of ancient and modern republics had taught them that many of the evils which these republics had suffered arose from the want of a certain balance and mutual control indispensable to a wise administration; they were convinced that popular assemblies are frequently misguided by ignorance, by sudden impulses, and the intrigues of ambitious men, and that some firm barrier against these operations was necessary; they, therefore, instituted your Senate, and the benefits we have experienced have fully justified their conceptions. . . .

Gentlemen, in their reasoning, have placed the interests of the several States and those of the United States in contrast; this is not a fair view of the subject; they must necessarily be involved in each other. What we apprehend is that some sinister prejudice, or some prevailing passion, may assume the form of a genuine interest. The influence of these is as powerful as the most permanent conviction of the public good; and against this influence we ought to provide. The local interests of a State ought in every case to give way to the interests of the Union, for when a sacrifice of one or the other is necessary, the former becomes only an apparent, partial interest, and should yield, on the principle that the small good ought never to oppose the great one. When you assemble from your several counties in the Legislature, were every member to be guided only by the apparent interests of his county, government would be impracticable. There must be a perpetual accommodation and sacrifice of local advantages to general expediency; but the spirit of a mere popular assembly would rarely be actuated by this important principle. It is therefore absolutely necessary that the Senate should be so formed as to be unbiased by false conceptions of the real interests, or undue attachment to the apparent good of their several States.

Gentlemen indulge too many unreasonable apprehensions of danger to the State governments; they seem to suppose that the moment you put men into a national council, they become corrupt and tyrannical, and lose all their affection for their fellow-citizens. But can we imagine that the Senators will ever be so insensible of their own advantage as to sacrifice the genuine interest of their constituents? The State governments are essentially necessary to the form and spirit of the general system. As long, therefore, as Congress has a full conviction of this necessity, they must, even upon principles purely national, have as firm an attachment to the one as to the other. This conviction can never leave them, unless they become madmen. While the Constitution continues to be read, and its principle known, the States must, by every rational man, be considered as essential, component parts of the Union; and therefore the idea of sacrificing the former to the latter is wholly inadmissible.

The objectors do not advert to the natural strength and resources of State governments, which will ever give them an important superiority over the general government. If we compare the nature of their different powers, or the means of popular influence which each possesses, we shall find the advantage entirely on the side of the States. This consideration, important as it is, seems to have been little attended to. The aggregate number of Representatives throughout the States may be two thousand. Their personal influence will, therefore, be proportionably more extensive than that of one or two hundred men in Congress. The

State establishments of civil and military officers of every description, infinitely surpassing in number any possible correspondent establishments in the general government, will create such an extent and complication of attachments, as will ever secure the predilection and support of the people. Whenever, therefore, Congress shall meditate any infringement of the State Constitutions, the great body of the people will naturally take part with their domestic representatives. Can the general government withstand such a united opposition? Will the people suffer themselves to be stripped of their privileges? Will they suffer their Legislatures to be reduced to a shadow and a name? The idea is shocking to common sense.

From the circumstances already explained, and many others which might be mentioned, results a complicated, irresistible check, which must ever support the existence and importance of the State governments. The danger, if any exists, flows from an opposite source. The probable evil is that the general government will be too dependent on the State Legislatures, too much governed by their prejudices, and too obsequious to their humors - that the States, with every power in their hands, will make encroachments on the national authority, till the Union is weakened and dissolved.

Every member must have been struck with an observation of a gentleman from Albany. Do what you will, says he, local prejudices and opinions will go into the government. What! Shall we then form a Constitution to cherish and strengthen these prejudices? Shall we confirm the distemper instead of remedying it. It is undeniable that there must be a control somewhere. Either the general interest is to control the particular interests, or the contrary. If the former, then certainly the government ought to be so framed as to render the power of control efficient to all intents and purposes; if the latter, a striking absurdity follows; the controlling powers must be as numerous as the varying interests, and the operations of the government must therefore cease, for the moment you accommodate these different interests, which is the only way to set the government in motion, you establish a controlling power. Thus, whatever constitutional provisions are made to the contrary, every government will be at last driven to the necessity of subjecting the partial to the universal interest. The gentlemen ought always, in their reasoning, to distinguish between the real, genuine good of a State, and the opinions and prejudices which may prevail respecting it; the latter may be opposed to the general good, and consequently ought to be sacrificed; the former is so involved in it that it never can be sacrificed.

There are certain social principles in human nature from which we may draw the most solid conclusions with respect to the conduct of individuals and of communities. We love our families more than our neighbors; we love our neighbors more than our countrymen in general. The human affections, like the solar heat, lose their intensity as they depart from the center, and become languid in proportion to the expansion of the circle on which they act. On these principles, the attachment of the individual will be first and forever secured by the State governments; they will be a mutual protection and support. Another source of influence, which has already been pointed out, is the various official connections in the States. Gentlemen endeavor to evade the force of this by saying that these offices will be insignificant. This is by no means true. The State officers will ever be important, because they are necessary and useful. Their powers are such as are extremely interesting to the people - such as affect their property, their liberty, and life. What is more important than the administration of justice and the execution of the civil and criminal laws? Can the State governments become insignificant while they have the power of raising money independently and without control? If they are really useful - if they are calculated to promote the essential interests of the people - they must have their confidence and support. The States can never lose their powers till the whole people of America are robbed of their liberties. These must go together; they must support each other or meet one common fate. On the gentleman's principle, we may safely trust the State governments, though we have no means of resisting them; but we cannot confide in the national government, though we have an effectual constitutional guard against every encroachment. This is the essence of their argument, and it is false and fallacious beyond conception.

With regard to the jurisdiction of the two governments, I shall certainly admit that the Constitution ought to be so formed as not to prevent the States from providing for their own existence; and I maintain that it is so formed, and that their power of providing for themselves is sufficiently established. This is conceded by one gentleman, and in the next breath the concession is retracted. He says Congress has but one exclusive right in taxation - that of duties on imports; certainly, then, their other powers are only concurrent. But to take off the force of this obvious conclusion, he immediately says that the laws of the United States are supreme and that where there is one supreme there cannot be a concurrent authority, and further, that where the laws of the Union are supreme, those of the States must be subordinate, because there cannot be two supremes. This is curious sophistry. That two supreme powers cannot act together is false. They are inconsistent only when they are aimed at each other or at one indivisible object. The laws of the United States are supreme, as to all their proper, con-

stitutional objects; the laws of the States are supreme in the
same way. These supreme laws may act on different objects
without clashing; or they may operate on different parts of
the same common object with perfect harmony. Suppose
both governments should lay a tax of a penny on a certain
article; has not each an independent and uncontrollable
power to collect its own tax? The meaning of the maxim,
there cannot be two supremes, is simply this - two powers
cannot be supreme over each other. This meaning is entirely perverted by the gentlemen. But, it is said, disputes
between collectors are to be referred to the Federal courts.
This is again wandering in the field of conjecture. But suppose the fact is certain; is it not to be presumed that they
will express the true meaning of the Constitution and the
laws? Will they not be bound to consider the concurrent
jurisdiction, to declare that both the taxes shall have equal
operation, that both the powers, in that respect, are sovereign and co-extensive? If they transgress their duty, we are
to hope that they will be punished. Sir, we can reason from
probabilities alone. When we leave common sense, and give
ourselves up to conjecture, there can be no certainty, no
security in our reasonings.

I imagine I have stated to the committee abundant reasons
to prove the entire safety of the State governments and of
the people. I would go into a more minute consideration of
the nature of the concurrent jurisdiction, and the operation
of the laws in relation to revenue, but at present I feel too
much indisposed to proceed. I shall, with leave of the
committee, improve another opportunity of expressing to
them more fully my ideas on this point. I wish the committee to remember that the Constitution under examination is framed upon truly republican principles, and that, as
it is expressly designed to provide for the common protection and the general welfare of the United States, it must be

utterly repugnant to this Constitution to subvert the State governments or oppress the people.

Afterward

On July 25, 1788, swayed by the force of Alexander Hamilton's arguments, the New York State Convention ratified the proposed Constitution by three votes. Hamilton went on to serve in the Continental Congress (1788-89), and as President Washington's Secretary of the Treasury (1789-1795). He returned to New York in 1796 to lead the Federalist Party against the Republican (formerly the Anti-Federalist) Party, led by his political foe, Aaron Burr. The bitter political rivalry between the two ended in a duel between Hamilton and then Vice President of the United States, Aaron Burr, on July 11, 1804. Alexander Hamilton died later that day of his wounds.

Selected Reading

Hacker, Louis, *Alexander Hamilton in the American Tradition*, 1957.

Hecht, Marie, *Odd Destiny: The Life of Alexander Hamilton*, 1982.

Lodge, Henry Cabot, *Alexander Hamilton*, 1882.

Mitchell, Broadus, *Alexander Hamilton: The National Adventure*, 1962.

Morris, Richard, Editor, *Alexander Hamilton and the Founding of the Nation*, 1957.

Oliver, Frederick, *Alexander Hamilton*, 1923.

Rossiter, Clinton, *Alexander Hamilton and the Constitution*, 1964.

Schachner, Nathan, *Alexander Hamilton*, 1946.

Stourzh, Gerald, *Alexander Hamilton and the Idea of Republican Government*, 1970.

Vandenberg, Arthur, *The Greatest American: Alexander Hamilton*, 1911.

Andrew Hamilton
The Trial Of John Peter Zenger
August 4, 1735

It is ordered that the Sheriff for the City of New York do forthwith apprehend John Peter Zenger and commit him to prison, for printing and publishing several seditious libels in his newspaper, the New York Weekly Journal, as having in it many things tending to raise factions and tumults among the people of this Province, inflaming their minds with contempt of His Majesty's Government and greatly disturbing the peace thereof. **- The Arrest Warrant For John Peter Zenger**

John Peter Zenger, born in Germany in 1697 and immigrating to America in 1710, was the publisher of the New York *Weekly Journal.* In 1732 King George II appointed William Cosby Royal Governor of the Colony of New York. On November 17, 1734, Zenger, whose editorials had been highly critical of Cosby, was imprisoned on a charge of printing false, scandalous, and seditious libels.

Zenger's bail was set at ten times his worth, and the court appointed a lawyer loyal to the Government to represent him. Zenger wrote to Philadelphia lawyer Andrew Hamilton, pleading with him to take up his defense.

Born in 1656 in Scotland and educated as a lawyer in England, Andrew Hamilton immigrated to America in the early 1700's. He had served as William Penn's personal lawyer, as the Pennsylvania Attorney General, and as the Speaker of the Pennsylvania Assembly. Hamilton, almost eighty, immediately agreed to take Zenger's case.

The trial was held on August 4, 1734. Just after the jury was seated, Hamilton walked into the courtroom and displaced Zenger's court-appointed lawyer. He turned the tables on the prosecution and argued that Governor Cosby should be on trial for censorship. He closed his defense of John Peter Zenger with this landmark speech.

Andrew Hamilton

May it please Your Honors, I agree with [the prosecuting] attorney that government is a sacred thing, but I differ very widely from him when he would insinuate that the just complaints of a number of men, who suffer under a bad administration, is libeling that administration. Had I believed that to be law, I should not have given the court the trouble of hearing anything that I could say in this cause. . . .

I was in hopes as that terrible court where those dreadful judgments were given and that law established, which [the prosecuting] attorney has produced for authorities to support this cause, was long ago laid aside as the most dangerous court to the liberties of the people of England that ever was known in that kingdom, that [the prosecuting] attorney, knowing this, would not have attempted to set up a Star Chamber here, nor to make their judgments a precedent to us; for it is well known that what would have been judged treason in those days for a man to speak, I think, has since not only been practiced as lawful, but the contrary doctrine has been held to be law.

There is heresy in law as well as in religion, and both have changed very much; and we well know that it is not two centuries ago that a man would have been burned as a heretic for owning such opinions in matters of religion as are publicly written and printed at this day. They were fallible men, it seems, and we take the liberty, not only to differ from them in religious opinion, but to condemn them and their opinions too; and I must presume that in taking these freedoms in thinking and speaking about matters of faith or religion, we are in the right, for, though it is said there are very great liberties of this kind taken in New York, yet I have heard of no information preferred by [the prosecuting] attorney for any offenses of this sort. From which I think it is pretty clear that in New York a man may make very free with his God, but he must take special care what he says of his Governor. It is agreed upon by all men that this is a reign of liberty, and while men keep within the bounds of truth, I hope they may with safety both speak and write their sentiments of the conduct of men of power - I mean of that part of their conduct only which affects the liberty or property of the people under their administration - were this to be denied, then the next step may make them slaves. For what notions can be entertained of slavery beyond that of suffering the greatest injuries and oppressions without the liberty of complaining, or if they do, to be destroyed, body and estate, for so doing?

It is said, and insisted upon by [the prosecuting] attorney, that government is a sacred thing, that it is to be supported and reverenced; it is government that protects our persons and estates, that prevents treasons, murders, robberies, riots, and all the train of evils that overturn kingdoms and states and ruin particular persons. And if those in the administration, especially the supreme magistrates, must have all their conduct censured by private men, government cannot subsist. This is called a licentiousness not to be tolerated. It is said that it brings the rulers of the people into contempt so that their authority is not regarded, and so that in the end the laws cannot be put in execution. These, I say, and such as these, are the general topics insisted upon by men in power and their advocates. But I wish it might be considered at the same time how often it has happened that the abuse of power has been the primary cause of these evils, and that it was the injustice and oppression of these great men which has commonly brought them into contempt with the people. The craft and art of such men are great, and who that is the least acquainted with history or with law can be ignorant of the specious pretenses which have often been made use of by men in power to introduce arbitrary rule and destroy the liberties of a free people. . . .

This is the second information for libeling of a governor that I have known in America. And the first, though it may look like a romance, yet, as it is true, I will beg leave to mention it. Governor Nicholson, who happened to be offended with one of his clergy, met him one day upon the road, and, as it was usual with him (under the protection of his commission), used the poor parson with the worst of language, threatened to cut off his ears, slit his nose, and, at last, to shoot him through the head. The parson, being a reverend man, continued all this time uncovered in the heat of the sun until he found an opportunity to fly for it, and coming to a neighbor's house felt himself very ill of a fever, and immediately wrote for a doctor. And that his physician might be the better judge of his distemper, he acquainted him with the usage he had received, concluding that the Governor was certainly mad, for that no man in his senses would have behaved in that manner. The doctor, unhappily, showed the parson's letter; the Governor came to hear of it, and so an information was preferred against the poor man for saying he believed the Governor was mad; and it was laid in the information to be false, scandalous, and wicked, and written with intent to move sedition among the people and bring his Excellency into contempt. But, by an order from the late Queen Anne, there was a stop put to the prosecution, with sundry others set on foot by the same Governor against gentlemen of the greatest worth and honor in that government.

And may not I be allowed, after all this, to say that, by a little countenance, almost anything which a man writes may, with the help of that useful term of art called an innuendo, be construed to be a libel, according to [the prosecuting] attorney's definition of it - that whether the words are spoken of a person of a public character or of a private man, whether dead or living, good or bad, true or false, all make a libel, for, according to [the prosecuting] attorney, after a man hears a writing read, or reads and repeats it, or laughs at it, they are all punishable. . . .

If a libel is understood in the large and unlimited sense urged by [the prosecuting] attorney, there is scarce a writing I know that may not be called a libel, or scarce any person safe from being called to account as a libeler, for Moses, meek as he was, libeled Cain, and who is it that has not libeled the devil? . . . How must a man speak or write, or what must he hear, read, or sing? Or when must he laugh, so as to be secure from being taken up as a libeler? I sincerely believe that were some persons to go through the streets of New York nowadays and read a part of the Bible, if it were not known to be such, [the prosecuting] attorney, with the help of his innuendoes, would easily turn it into a libel. . . .

Gentlemen, the danger is great in proportion to the mischief that may happen through our too-great credulity. A proper confidence in a court is commendable, but as the verdict (whatever it is) will be yours, you ought to refer no part of your duty to the discretion of other persons. If you should be of opinion that there is no falsehood in Mr. Zenger's papers, you will, nay (pardon me for the expression), you ought to say so, because you do not know whether others (I mean the court) may be of that opinion. It is your right to do so, and there is much depending upon your resolution, as well as upon your integrity.

The loss of liberty to a generous mind is worse than death; and yet we know there have been those in all ages who, for the sake of preferment or some imaginary honor, have freely lent a helping hand to oppress, nay, to destroy, their country. This brings to my mind that saying of the immortal Brutus, when he looked upon the creatures of Caesar, who were very great men, but by no means good men. *You Romans*, said Brutus, *if yet I may call you so, consider what you are doing; remember that you are assisting Caesar to forge those very chains which one day he will make yourselves wear.* This is what every man that values freedom ought to consider; he should act by judgment and not by affection or self-interest, for where those prevail, no ties of either country or kindred are regarded, as, upon the other hand, the man who loves his country prefers its liberty to all other considerations, well knowing that without liberty life is a misery. . . .

Power may justly be compared to a great river; while kept within its bounds, it is both beautiful and useful, but when it overflows its banks, it is then too impetuous to be stemmed; it bears down all before it, and brings destruction and desolation wherever it comes. If, then, this be the nature of power, let us at least do our duty, and, like wise men who value freedom, use our utmost care to support liberty, the only bulwark against lawless power, which, in all ages, has sacrificed to its wild lust and boundless ambition the blood of the best men that ever lived.

I hope to be pardoned, sir, for my zeal upon this occasion. It is an old and wise caution that *when our neighbor's house is on fire, we ought to take care of our own.* For though, blessed be God, I live in a government where liberty is well understood and freely enjoyed, yet experience has shown us all (I am sure it has to me) that a bad precedent in one government is soon set up for an authority in another; and therefore I cannot but think it mine and every honest man's duty that, while we pay all due obedience to men in authority, we ought, at the same time, to be upon our guard against power wherever we apprehend that it may affect ourselves or our fellow subjects.

I am truly very unequal to such an undertaking, on many accounts. And you see I labor under the weight of many years and am borne down with great infirmities of body; yet old and weak as I am, I should think it my duty, if required, to go to the utmost part of the land, where my service could be of any use in assisting to quench the flame of prosecutions upon informations set on foot by the government to deprive a people of the right of remonstrating, and complaining too, of the arbitrary attempts of men in power. Men who injure and oppress the people under their administration provoke them to cry out and complain, and then make that very complaint the foundation for new oppressions and prosecutions. I wish I could say there were no instances of this kind. But, to conclude, the question before the court, and you, gentlemen of the jury, is not of small nor private concern; it is not the cause of a poor printer, nor of New York alone, which you are now trying. No! It may in its consequence affect every free man that lives under a British government on the main continent of America. It is the best cause - it is the cause of liberty - and I make no doubt but your upright conduct this day will not only entitle you to the love and esteem of your fellow citizen, but every man who prefers freedom to a life of slavery will bless and honor you as men who have baffled the attempt of tyranny, and, by an impartial and uncorrupt verdict, have laid a noble foundation for securing to ourselves, our posterity, and our neighbors that to which nature and the laws of our country have given us a right - the liberty of both exposing and opposing arbitrary power (in these parts of the world at least) by speaking and writing truth.

Andrew Hamilton

Afterward

In 1736 Zenger published *A Brief Narrative of the Trial of John Peter Zenger*, in which he described what happened after Andrew Hamilton's closing arguments, *The jury withdrew and in a small time returned and being asked by the Clerk whether they were agreed on their verdict of whether I was guilty printing and publishing libels. They answered "Not Guilty," upon which there were three Huzzas! from the people. I was discharged from my imprisonment.*

Alexander Hamilton died on August 4, 1741.

Selected Reading

Konkle, Burton A., *The Life of Andrew Hamilton*, 1972.
Putnam, William L., *John Peter Zenger and the Fundamental Freedom*, 1997.
Rutherford, Livingston, *John Peter Zenger*, 1964.

John Hancock
The Boston Massacre Remembered
March 5, 1774

Heard the oration pronounced by John Hancock in commemoration on the Massacre. An elegant, . . . spirited performance [delivered before] a vast crowd. . . . Many of the sentiments came with great propriety from him. His invective, particularly against a preference of riches to virtue, came from him with a singular dignity and grace.
- The Diary of John Adams, March 5, 1774

John Hancock, Jr. was born on January 23, 1737 in North Braintree, Massachusetts. After the death of his father in 1744, he was adopted by his uncle, Thomas Hancock. He studied at Harvard College, worked at the offices of Hancock & Company, and was tutored by Sons of Liberty founders Samuel Adams and John Otis.

In 1765 the British Parliament passed into law the Stamp Act, which for the first time directly taxed Americans. Hancock joined with Adams and Otis in active political opposition to the Stamp Act, which was repealed in 1766. In 1767 Parliament passed the Townshend Acts, which were to tax American imports and exports. On the night of May 9, 1768, John Hancock's ship *Liberty* arrived in Boston from Madeira carrying a cargo of wine. The next morning British tax officials found her holds unloaded - her vanished cargo untaxed. On June 10 the *Liberty* was seized and Hancock was hauled into Tax Court. Boston's Sons of Liberty took their protests to the street. In court, John Adams defended Hancock and demanded the return of the *Liberty*. A judge found against Hancock. The British Army marched into Boston in October 1768. An escalating series of street clashes led up to the Boston Massacre. Each year, on the anniversary of the Massacre, a commemoration is held. On the fourth anniversary, March 5, 1774, John Hancock delivered this landmark speech.

John Hancock

I have always, from my earliest youth, rejoiced in the felicity of my fellow-men, and have ever considered it as the indispensable duty of every member of society to promote, as far as in him lies, the prosperity of every individual, but more especially of the community to which he belongs, and also as a faithful subject of the State, to use his utmost endeavors to detect, and having detected, strenuously to oppose, every traitorous plot which its enemies may devise for its destruction. Security to the persons and properties of the governed is so obviously the design and end of civil government that to attempt a logical proof of it would be like burning tapers at noonday to assist the sun in enlightening the world; and it cannot be either virtuous or honorable to attempt to support a government of which this is not the great and principal basis; and it is to the last degree vicious and infamous to attempt to support a government which manifestly tends to render the persons and properties of the governed insecure.

Some boast of being friends to government; I am a friend to righteous government, to a government founded upon the principles of reason and justice; but I glory in publicly avowing my eternal enmity to tyranny. Is the present system, which the British administration have adopted for the government of the colonies, a righteous government, or is it tyranny? Here suffer me to ask (and would to Heaven there could be an answer) what tenderness, what regard, respect, or consideration has Great Britain shown, in their late transactions, for the security of the persons or properties of the inhabitants of the colonies? Or rather what have they omitted doing to destroy that security? They have declared that they have ever had, and of right ought ever to have, full power to make laws of sufficient validity to bind the colonies in all cases whatever. They have exercised this pretended right by imposing a tax on us without our consent; and lest we should show some reluctance at parting with our property, her fleets and armies are sent to enforce their mad pretensions. The town of Boston, ever faithful to the British Crown, has been invested by a British fleet; the troops of George III have crossed the wide Atlantic, not to engage an enemy, but to assist a band of traitors in trampling on the rights and liberties of his most loyal subjects in America - those rights and liberties which, as a father, he ought ever to regard, and as a King, he is bound, in honor, to defend from violation, even at the risk of his own life.

Let not the history of the illustrious house of Brunswick inform posterity, that a King, descended from that glorious monarch, George II, once sent his British subjects to conquer and enslave his subjects in America. But be perpetual infamy entailed upon that villain who dared to advise his master to such execrable measures, for it was easy to foresee the consequences which so naturally followed upon sending troops into America, to enforce obedience to acts of the British Parliament, which neither God nor man ever empowered them to make.

It was reasonable to expect that troops, who knew the errand they were sent upon, would treat the people whom they were to subjugate with a cruelty and haughtiness which too often buries the honorable character of a soldier in the disgraceful name of an unfeeling ruffian. The troops, upon their first arrival, took possession of our senate house, and pointed their cannon against the judgment hall, and even continued them there whilst the supreme court of judicature for this province was actually sitting there to decide upon the lives and fortunes of the King's subjects. Our streets nightly resounded with the noise of riot and debauchery, our peaceful citizens were hourly exposed to shameful insults, and often felt the effects of their violence and outrage. But this was not all; as though they thought it not enough to violate our civil rights, they endeavored to deprive us of the enjoyment of our religious privileges, to vitiate our morals, and thereby render us worthy of destruction.

Hence the rude din of arms which broke in upon your solemn devotions in your temples, on that day hallowed by Heaven, and set apart by God himself for His peculiar worship. Hence, impious oaths and blasphemies so often tortured your unaccustomed ears. Hence, all the arts which idleness and luxury could invent were used to betray our youth of one sex into extravagance and effeminacy, and of the other, to infamy and ruin, and did they not succeed but too well? Did not a reverence for religion sensibly decay? Did not our infants almost learn to lisp out curses before they knew their horrid import? Did not our youth forget they were Americans, and regardless of the admonitions of the wise and aged servilely copy from their tyrants those vices which finally must overthrow the empire of Great Britain? And must I be compelled to acknowledge that even the noblest, fairest part of all the lower creation did not entirely escape the cursed snare? When virtue has once erected her throne in the female breast, it is upon so solid a basis that nothing is able to expel the heavenly inhabitant. But have there not been some, few indeed, I hope, whose youth and inexperience have rendered them a prey to wretches whom, upon the least reflection, they would have despised and hated as foes to God and their country? I fear there have been some such unhappy instances, or why have I seen an honest father clothed with shame, or why a virtuous mother drowned in tears?

But I forbear, and come reluctantly to that dismal night when in such quick succession we felt the extremes of grief, astonishment, and rage, when Heaven in anger, for a dreadful moment, suffered hell to take the reins, when Satan with his chosen band opened the sluices of New England's blood, and sacrilegiously polluted our land with the dead bodies of her guiltless sons! Let this sad tale of death never be told without a tear; let not the heaving bosom cease to burn with manly indignation at the barbarous story, through the long tracts of future time. Let every parent tell the shameful story to his listening children until tears of pity glisten in their eyes, and boiling passions shake their tender frames; and whilst the anniversary of that ill-fated night is kept a jubilee in the grim courts of pandemonium, let all America join in one common prayer to Heaven, that the inhuman, unprovoked murders of the fifth of March, 1770, planned by Hillsborough and a knot of treacherous knaves in Boston, and executed by the cruel hand of Preston and his sanguinary coadjutors, may ever stand on history without a parallel.

But what, my countrymen, withheld the ready arm of vengeance from executing instant justice on the vile assassins? Perhaps you feared promiscuous carnage might ensue, and that the innocent might share the fate of those who had performed the infernal deed? But were not all guilty? Were you not too tender of the lives of those who came to fix a yoke on your necks? But I must not too severely blame a fault which great souls only can commit. May that magnificence of spirit which scorns the low pursuit of malice, may that generous compassion which often preserves from ruin, even a guilty villain, forever actuate the noble bosoms of Americans!

But let not the miscreant host vainly imagine that we feared their arms. No, them we despised - we dread nothing but slavery. Death is the creature of a poltroon's brains; 'tis immortality to sacrifice ourselves for the salvation of our country. We fear not death. That gloomy night, the pale-faced moon, and the affrighted stars that hurried through the sky, can witness that we fear not death. Our hearts which, at the recollection, glow with rage that four revolving years have scarcely taught us to restrain, can witness that we fear not death; and happy it is for those who dared to insult us that their naked bodies are not now piled up, an everlasting monument to Massachusetts' bravery. But they retired, they fled, and in that flight they found their only safety.

We then expected that the hand of public justice would soon inflict that punishment upon the murderers, which by the laws of God and man they had incurred. But let the unbiased pen of a Robertson, or perhaps of some equally famed American, conduct this trial before the great tribunal of succeeding generations. And though the murderers may escape the just resentment of an outraged people; though drowsy justice, intoxicated by the poisonous draught prepared for her cup still nods upon her rotten seat, yet be assured such complicated crimes will meet their due reward. Tell me, ye bloody butchers! ye villains high and low! ye wretches who contrived, as well as you who executed the inhuman deed! do you not feel the goads and stings of conscious guilt pierce through your savage bosoms? Though some of you may think yourselves exalted to a height that bids defiance to human justice, and others shroud yourselves beneath the mask of hypocrisy, and build your hopes of safety on the low arts of cunning, chicanery, and falsehood, yet do you not sometimes feel the gnawings of that worm which never dies? Do not the injured shades of

Maverick, Gray, Caldwell, Attucks, and Carr attend you in your solitary walks; arrest you even in the midst of your debaucheries, and fill even your dreams with terror? But if the unappeased names of the dead should not disturb their murderers, yet surely even your obdurate hearts must shrink, and your guilty blood must chill within your rigid veins, when you behold the miserable Monk, the wretched victim of your savage cruelty. Observe his tottering knees, which scarce sustain his wasted body; look on his haggard eyes; mark well the deathlike paleness on his fallen cheek, and tell me, does not the sight plant daggers in your souls? Unhappy Monk! Cut off, in the gay morn of manhood, from all the joys which sweeten life, doomed to drag on a pitiful existence, without even a hope to taste the pleasures of returning health! Yet, Monk, thou livest not in vain; thou livest a warning to thy country, which sympathizes with thee in thy sufferings; thou livest an affecting, an alarming instance of the unbounded violence which lust of power, assisted by a standing army, can lead a traitor to commit.

For us he bled and now languishes. The wounds by which he is tortured to a lingering death were aimed at our country! Surely the meek-eyed Charity can never behold such sufferings with indifference. Nor can her lenient hand forbear to pour oil and wine into these wounds, and to assuage, at least, what it can never heal.

Patriotism is ever united with humanity and compassion. This noble affection, which impels us to sacrifice everything dear, even life itself, to our country, involves in it a common sympathy and tenderness for every citizen, and must ever have a particular feeling for one who suffers in a public cause. Thoroughly persuaded of this, I need not add a word to engage your compassion and bounty toward a fellow-citizen who, with long-protracted anguish, falls a victim to the relentless rage of our common enemies.

Ye dark, designing knaves, ye murderers, parricides! How dare you tread upon the earth which has drank in the blood of slaughtered innocents, shed by your wicked hands? How dare you breathe that air which wafted to the ear of Heaven the groans of those who fell a sacrifice to your accursed ambition? But if the laboring earth doth not expand her jaws, if the air you breathe is not commissioned to be the minister of death, yet, hear it and tremble! The eye of Heaven penetrates the darkest chambers of the soul, traces the leading clue through all the labyrinths which your industrious folly has devised; and you, however you may have screened yourselves from human eyes, must be arraigned, must lift your hands, red with the blood of those whose death you have procured, at the tremendous bar of God!

But I gladly quit the gloomy theme of death, and leave you to improve the thought of that important day when our naked souls must stand before that Being from whom nothing can be hid. I would not dwell too long upon the horrid effects which have already followed from quartering regular troops in this town. Let our misfortunes teach posterity to guard against such evils for the future. Standing armies are sometimes (I would by no means say generally, much less universally) composed of persons who have rendered themselves unfit to live in civil society - who have no other motives of conduct than those which a desire of the present gratification of their passions suggests, who have no property in any country - men who have given up their own liberties, and envy those who enjoy liberty, who are equally indifferent to the glory of a George or a Louis, who, for the addition of one penny a day to their wages, would desert from the Christian cross and fight under the crescent of the Turkish sultan. From such men as these, what has not a State to fear? With such as these, usurping Caesar passed the Rubicon; with such as these, he humbled mighty Rome, and forced the mistress of the world to own a master in a traitor. These are the men whom sceptred robbers now employ to frustrate the designs of God, and render vain the bounties which his gracious hand pours indiscriminately upon his creatures. By these, the miserable slaves of Turkey, Persia, and many other extensive countries are rendered truly wretched, though their air is salubrious and their soil luxuriously fertile. By these, France and Spain, though blessed by nature with all that administers to the convenience of life, have been reduced to that contemptible state in which they now appear; and by these, Britain - but if I was possessed of the gift of prophecy, I dare not, except by divine command, unfold the leaves on which the destiny of that once powerful kingdom is inscribed.

But since standing armies are so hurtful to a State, perhaps my countrymen may demand some substitute, some other means of rendering us secure against the incursions of a foreign enemy. But can you be one moment at a loss? Will not a well disciplined militia afford you ample security against foreign foes? We want not courage; it is discipline alone in which we are exceeded by the most formidable troops that ever trod the earth. Surely our hearts flutter no more at the sound of war than did those of the immortal band of Persia, the Macedonian phalanx, the invincible Roman legions, the Turkish janissaries, the gens d'armes of France, or the well-known grenadiers of Britain. A well-disciplined militia is a safe, an honorable guard to a community like this, whose inhabitants are by nature brave, and are laudably tenacious of that freedom in which they were born. From a well-regulated militia we have nothing to fear; their interest is the same with that of the State. When a country is invaded, the militia are ready to appear in its defense; they march into the field with that fortitude which a consciousness of the justice of their cause inspires; they do not jeopard their lives for a master who considers them only as the instruments of his ambition, and whom they regard only as the daily dispenser of the scanty pittance of bread and water. No! they fight for their houses, their lands, for their wives, their children, for all who claim the tenderest names and are held dearest in their hearts; they fight pro aris et focis [for their altars and their firesides], for their liberty and for themselves and for their God. And let it not offend if I say that no militia ever appeared in more flourishing condition than that of this province now doth, and, pardon me if I say, of this town in particular. I mean not to boast; I would not excite envy, but manly emulation.

We have all one common cause; let it, therefore, be our only contest, who shall most contribute to the security of the liberties of America. And may the same kind Providence which has watched over this country from her infant state still enable us to defeat our enemies. I cannot here forbear noticing the signal manner in which the designs of those who wish not well to us have been discovered. The dark deeds of a treacherous cabal have been brought to public view. You now know the serpents who, whilst cherished in your bosoms, were darting their envenomed stings into the vitals of the Constitution. But the representatives of the people have fixed a mark on these ungrateful monsters, which, though it may not make them so secure as Cain of old, yet renders them at least as infamous. Indeed, it would be affrontive to the tutelar deity of this country even to despair of saving it from all the snares which human policy can lay.

True it is that the British ministry have annexed a salary to the office of the governor of this province, to be paid out of a revenue raised in America without our consent. They have attempted to render our courts of justice the instruments of extending the authority of acts of the British Parliament over this colony, by making the judges dependent on the British administration for their support. But this people will never be enslaved with their eyes open. The moment they knew that the governor was not such a governor as the charter of the province points out, he lost his power of hurting them. They were alarmed; they suspected him, have guarded against him, and he has found that a wise and a brave people, when they know their danger, are fruitful in expedients to escape it. . . . Great expectations were also formed from the artful scheme of allowing the East India Company to export tea to America upon their own account. This certainly, had it succeeded, would have effected the purpose of the contrivers, and gratified the most sanguine wishes of our adversaries. We soon should have found our trade in the hands of foreigners, and taxes imposed on everything we consumed; nor would it have been strange if, in a few years, a company in London should have purchased an exclusive right of trading to America. But their plot was soon discovered. The people soon were aware of the poison which, with so much craft and subtlety, had been concealed. Loss and disgrace ensued, and perhaps this long-concerted masterpiece of policy may issue in the total disuse of tea in this country, which will eventually be the saving of the lives and the estates of thousands.

Yet, while we rejoice that the adversary has not hitherto prevailed against us, let us by no means put off the harness. Restless malice and disappointed ambition will still suggest new measures to our inveterate enemies. Therefore, let us also be ready to take the field whenever danger calls; let us be united and strengthen the hands of each other by promoting a general union among us. Much has been done by the Committees of Correspondence, for this and the other towns of this province, toward uniting the inhabitants; let them still go on and prosper. Much has been done by the Committees of Correspondence for the Houses of Assembly, in this and our sister colonies, for uniting the inhabitants of the whole continent, for the security of their common interest. May success ever attend their generous endeavors. But permit me here to suggest a general congress of deputies, from the several Houses of Assembly on the continent, as the most effectual method of establishing such a union as the present posture of our affairs requires. At such a congress, a firm foundation may be laid for the security of our rights and liberties; a system may be formed for our common safety, by a strict adherence to which we shall be able to frustrate any attempt to overthrow our constitution, restore peace and harmony to America, and secure honor and wealth to Great Britain, even against the inclinations of her ministers, whose duty it is to study her welfare. And we shall also free ourselves from those unmannerly pillagers who impudently tell us that they are licensed by an act of the British Parliament to thrust their dirty hands into the pockets of every American. But I trust the happy time will come when, with the besom of destruction, those noxious vermin will be swept forever from the streets of Boston.

Surely you never will tamely suffer this country to be a den of thieves. Remember, my friends, from whom you sprang. Let not a meanness of spirit, unknown to those whom you boast of as your fathers, excite a thought to the dishonor of your mothers. I conjure you, by all that is dear, by all that is honorable, by all that is sacred, not only that ye pray, but that ye act, that, if necessary, ye fight, and even die, for the prosperity of our Jerusalem. Break in sunder, with noble disdain, the bonds with which the Philistines have bound you. Suffer not yourselves to be betrayed, by the soft arts of luxury and effeminacy, into the pit digged for your destruction. Despise the glare of wealth. That people who pay greater respect to a wealthy villain than to an honest, upright man in poverty almost deserve to be enslaved; they plainly show that wealth, however it may be acquired, is, in their esteem, to be preferred to virtue.

But I thank God that America abounds in men who are superior to all temptation, whom nothing can divert from a steady pursuit of the interest of their country, who are at once its ornament and its safeguard. And sure I am I should not incur your displeasure, if I paid a respect, so justly due to their much honored characters, in this place. But when I name an Adams, such a numerous host of fellow patriots rush upon my mind that I fear it would take up too much of your time should I attempt to call over the illustrious roll. But your grateful hearts will point you to the men; and their revered names, in all succeeding times, shall grace the annals of America. From them let us, my friends, take example; from them let us catch the divine enthusiasm, and feel, each for himself, the godlike pleasure of diffusing happiness on all around us, of delivering the oppressed from the iron grasp of tyranny, of changing the hoarse complaints and bitter moans of wretched slaves into those cheerful songs which freedom and contentment must inspire. There is a heartfelt satisfaction in reflecting on our exertions for the public weal, which all the sufferings an enraged tyrant can inflict will never take away, which the ingratitude and reproaches of those whom we have saved from ruin cannot rob us of. The virtuous asserter of the rights of mankind merits a reward, which even a want of success in his endeavors to save his country (the heaviest misfortune which can befall a genuine patriot) cannot entirely prevent him from receiving. I have the most animating confidence that the present noble struggle for liberty will terminate gloriously for America. And let us play the man for our God, and for the cities of our God; while we are using the means in our power, let us humbly commit our righteous cause to the great Lord of the universe, who loveth righteousness and hateth iniquity. And having secured the approbation of our hearts by a faithful and unwearied discharge of our duty to our country, let us joyfully leave our concerns in the hands of Him who raiseth up and pulleth down the empires and kingdoms of the world as He pleases, and with cheerful submission to His sovereign will, devoutly say, *Although the fig-tree shall not blossom, neither shall fruit be in the vines; the labor of the olive shall fail, and the field shall yield no meat; the flock shall be cut off from the fold, and there shall be no herd in the stalls; yet we will rejoice in the Lord, we will joy in the God of our salvation.*

Afterward

John Hancock served as President of Massachusetts' Provisional Congress and President of the Second Continental Congress. Upon signing the Declaration of Independence, he is reported to have said of his bold signature, *There, I guess King George will be able to read that.* He later served as Massachusetts' Governor and President of the Federal Constitutional Convention. He died on October 8, 1793.

Selected Reading

Allan, Herbert S., *John Hancock, Patriot in Purple,* 1953.

Brandes, Paul D., *John Hancock's Life and Speeches: A Personalized Vision of the American Revolution,* 1996.

Fowler, William M., *The Baron of Beacon Hill: A Biography of John Hancock,* 1980.

Patrick Henry
Give Me Liberty Or Give Me Death!
March 23, 1775

The distinctions between New Englanders and Virginians are no more. I am not a Virginian but an American!

- Patrick Henry

The greatest orator that ever lived.

- Thomas Jefferson

Patrick Henry was born on May 29, 1738 in Hanover County, Virginia, the son of Judge John and Sarah (Winston) Henry. In 1760, he began to practice law. He fought over 1,185 lawsuits in the following three years, gaining a reputation as a powerful extemporaneous courtroom orator.

Patrick Henry was elected to Virginia's House of Burgesses in 1765, only days after the American Colonies learned that the British Parliament, in which no representative of colonial America had a vote, had passed into law the Stamp Act, which for the first time directly taxed Americans. His speeches against the Stamp Act, in particular, and the British Crown, in general, were reprinted in the Patriot newspapers of Boston, Philadelphia, and New York.

Henry became the leader of the independence faction in Virginia's House of Burgesses and a member of Virginia's Committee of Correspondence.

The Virginia Convention began on March 20, 1775 at St. John's Episcopal Church in Richmond. On the third day of the Convention, tired of proposals of compromise and negotiation, Patrick Henry introduced a resolution that Virginia immediately arm a militia to defend herself. He gave the following electrifying speech.

Patrick Henry

No man thinks more highly than I do of the patriotism, as well as the abilities, of the very worthy gentlemen who have just addressed the House. But different men often see the same subject in different lights and, therefore, I hope it will not be thought disrespectful to those gentleman if, entertaining as I do, opinions of a character very opposite to theirs, I should speak forth my sentiments freely, and without reserve. This is no time for ceremony. The question before the House is one of awful moment to this country. Should I keep back my opinions at such a time, through fear of giving offense, I should consider myself as guilty of treason towards my country, and of an act of disloyalty toward the majesty of heaven, which I revere above all earthly kings.

Mr. President, it is natural to man to indulge in the illusions of hope. We are apt to shut our eyes against a painful truth, and listen to the song of that siren, till she transforms us into beasts. Is this the part of wise men engaged in a great and arduous struggle for liberty? Are we disposed to be of the number of those who, having eyes, see not, and having ears, hear not, the things which so nearly concern their temporal salvation? For my part, whatever anguish of spirit it may cost, I am willing to know the whole truth, to know the worst, and to provide for it.

I have but one lamp by which my feet are guided, and that is the lamp of experience. I know of no way of judging of the future but by the past. And judging by the past, I wish to know what there has been in the conduct of the British ministry for the last ten years to justify those hopes with which gentlemen have been pleased to solace themselves and the House? Is it that insidious smile with which our petition has been lately received? Trust it not, sir - it will prove a snare to your feet. Suffer not yourselves to be betrayed with a kiss. Ask yourselves how this gracious reception of our petition comports with those warlike preparations which cover our waters and darken our land. Are fleets and armies necessary to a work of love and reconciliation? Have we shown ourselves so unwilling to be reconciled that force must be called in to win back our love? Let us not deceive ourselves, sir. These are the implements of war and subjugation - the last arguments to which kings resort. I ask gentlemen, sir, what means this martial array if its purpose be not to force us to submission? Can gentlemen assign any other possible motive for it? Has Great Britain any enemy in this quarter of the world to call for all this accumulation of navies and armies? No, sir, she has none. They are meant for us; they can be meant for no other. They are sent over to bind and rivet upon us those chains which the British ministry have been so long forging. And what have we to oppose them? Shall we try argument? Sir, we have been trying that for the last ten years. Have we anything new to offer upon the subject? Nothing. We have held the subject up in every light of which it is capable, but it has been all in vain. Shall we resort to entreaty and humble supplication? What terms shall we find that have not been already exhausted? Let us not, I beseech you, sir, deceive ourselves longer. Sir, we have done everything that could be done to avert the storm which is now coming on.

We have petitioned - we have remonstrated - we have supplicated - we have prostrated ourselves before the throne - and have implored its interposition to arrest the tyrannical hands of the ministry and the parliament. Our petitions have been slighted; our remonstrances have produced additional violence and insult; our supplications have been disregarded; and we have been spurned, with contempt, from the foot of the throne. In vain, after these things, may we indulge the fond hope of peace and reconciliation? There is no longer any room for hope. If we wish to be free - if we mean to preserve inviolate those inestimable privileges for which we have been so long contending - if we mean not basely to abandon the noble struggle in which we have been so long engaged, and which we have pledged ourselves never to abandon, until the glorious object of our contest shall be obtained - we must fight! I repeat, sir, we must fight! An appeal to arms and to the God of Hosts is all that is left us!

They tell us, sir, that we are weak - unable to cope with so formidable an adversary. But when shall we be stronger? Will it be the next week or the next year? Will it be when we are totally disarmed and when a British guard shall be stationed in every house? Shall we gather strength by ir-resolution and inaction? Shall we acquire the means of ef-fectual resistance by lying supinely on our backs and hug-ging the delusive phantom of hope until our enemies shall have bound us hand and foot? Sir, we are not weak, if we make a proper use of those means which the God of na-ture hath placed in our power. Three millions of people armed in the holy cause of liberty, and in such a country as that which we possess, are invincible by any force which our enemy can send against us. Besides, sir, we shall not fight our battles alone. There is a just God who presides over the destinies of nations, and who will raise up friends to fight our battles for us. The battle, sir, is not to the strong alone; it is to the vigilant, the active, the brave. Besides, sir, we have no election. If we are base enough to desire it, it is now too late to retire from the contest. There is no retreat but in submission and slavery! Our chains are forged. Their clanking may be heard on the plains of Boston! The war is inevitable - and let it come! I repeat, sir, let it come!

It is in vain, sir, to extenuate the matter. Gentlemen may cry, peace, peace - but there is no peace. The war is actually begun! The next gale that sweeps from the north will bring to our ears the clash of resounding arms! Our brethren are already in the field! Why stand we here idle? What is it that gentlemen wish? What would they have? Is life so dear, or peace so sweet, as to be purchased at the price of chains and slavery? Forbid it, Almighty God! I know not what course others may take but, as for me, give me liberty or give me death!

Afterward

The Virginia Convention approved Henry's *Call To Arms* Resolution. In 1776 the Virginia Convention drafted a new Constitution for Virginia and under that Constitution Henry was elected Virginia's Governor five times, serving 1776-1779 and 1784-1786. An opponent of strong centralized government, Patrick Henry refused to attend the Federal Constitutional Convention in 1787 and opposed the ratification of the Federal Constitution by Virginia. After the Constitution's adoption in 1788, Henry worked for the adoption of the 1791 Bill of Rights. In 1792 He retired from public life.

Patrick Henry died on June 6, 1799 at his home, *Red Hill*, in Charlotte County, Virginia.

Selected Reading

Axelrad, Jacob, *Patrick Henry, the Voice of Freedom*, 1947.
Beeman, Richard R., *Patrick Henry: A Biography*, 1974.
Campbell, Norine, *Patrick Henry: Patriot and Statesman*, 1969.
Carson, Julia M.H., *Son of Thunder: Patrick Henry*, 1945.
Mayer, Henry, *A Son of Thunder: Patrick Henry and the American Republic*, 1991.
McCants, David A., *Patrick Henry, the Orator*, 1990.
Willison, George F., *Patrick Henry and His World*, 1969.

Anne Hutchinson
The Heresy Trial Of Anne Hutchinson
November 8, 1637

Mistress Hutchinson, the sentence of this Court is that you are banished from out of our jurisdiction as being a women not fit for our society.   **- Governor John Winthrop**

Anne Marbury Hutchinson was a *Puritan*, a member of a non-conformist sect seeking to *purify* the Church of England. She was born on July 20, 1591 in Alford, England, the daughter of Francis Marbury and Bridget (Dryden) Marbury. On August 12, 1612, she married William Hutchinson. Persecuted in England for their religious beliefs, many Puritans emigrated in the early 1630's to the Massachusetts Bay Colony. Anne and her family arrived there on September 18, 1634.

The Puritan authorities of Massachusetts Bay were dedicated to a religious doctrine called *The Covenant of Works*, which stated that salvation or damnation was in God's hands. Anne Hutchinson believed in *The Covenant of Grace*, which stated that salvation or damnation was in the individual's hands. In 1635 she was ejected from the Boston Church and began to hold prayer services in her own home. The Puritan authorities condemned her meetings and, one by one, her supporters were banished from the Colony, reducing her support until she was almost alone.

Finally she herself was summoned to court, and her trial began on November 7, 1637. She was charged with holding *erroneous* religious views and practicing *sedition*. On November 8, knowing she would be found guilty and exiled, Anne Hutchinson stood up in court and, in one last act of defiance, replied to and refuted all the charges against her in this landmark speech.

When I was in old England, I was much troubled at the constitution of the Churches there, so far as I was ready to have joined to the Separation, whereupon I set apart a day for humiliation by myself, to seek direction from God, and then did God discover unto me the unfaithfulness of the Churches, and the danger of them, and that none of those Ministers could preach the Lord Jesus aright, for he had brought to my mind that in the [words of] John 4:3 - *Every spirit that confesseth not, that Jesus Christ is come in the flesh, is the spirit of Antichrist.* I marveled what this should mean, for I knew that neither Protestants nor Papists did deny that Christ was come in the flesh; and are the Turks then the only Antichrists?

Now I had none to open the Scripture to me but the Lord; he must be the Prophet. Then he brought to my mind another Scripture - *He that denies the Testament, denies the death of the Testator.* - from whence the Lord did let me see that everyone that did not preach the New Covenant denies the death of the Testator. Then it was revealed to me that the Ministers of England were these Antichrists, but I knew not how to bear this. I did in my heart rise up against it; then I begged of the Lord that this atheism might not be in my heart; after I had begged this light, a twelve month together, at last he let me see how I did oppose Christ Jesus, and he revealed to me that place in [Isaiah] 46:12, 13, and from thence showed me the atheism of my own heart, and how I did turn in upon a covenant of works, and did oppose Christ Jesus, from which time the Lord did discover to me all sorts of ministers, and how they taught, and to know what voice I heard - which was the voice of Moses, which of John Baptist, and which of Christ, the voice of my beloved, from the voice of strangers - and thenceforth I was the more careful whom I heard, for after our teacher, Mr.

Cotton, and my brother Wheelwright were put down, there was none in England that I durst hear. Then it pleased God to reveal himself to me in that of [Isaiah] 30:20 - *Though the Lord give thee the bread of adversity, etc., yet thine eyes shall see thy teachers.* - after this the Lord carrying Mr. Cotton to New England (at which I was much troubled), it was revealed to me that I must go thither also and that there I should be persecuted and suffer much trouble.

I will give you another Scripture, Jeremiah 46[:28] - *Fear not, Jacob, my servant, for I am with thee. I will make a full end of all the Nations, etc.* Then the Lord did reveal himself to me, sitting upon a Throne of Justice, and all the world appearing before him, and though I must come to New England, yet I must not fear nor be dismayed.

The Lord brought another Scripture to me, [Isaiah] 8:9 - *The Lord spake this to me with a strong hand, and instructed me that I should not walk in the way of this people, etc.* I will give you one place more which the Lord brought to me by immediate revelations, and that doth concern you all; it is in Daniel 6[:4] - *When the Presidents and Princes could find nothing against him, because he was faithful, they sought matter against him concerning the Law of his God, to cast him into the Lion's den; so it was revealed to me that they should plot against me, but the Lord bid me not to fear, for he that delivered Daniel, and the three children, his hand was not shortened.*

And see this Scripture fulfilled this day in mine eyes; therefore take heed what ye go about to do unto me, for you have no power over my body, neither can you do me any harm, for I am in the hands of the eternal Jehovah, my Savior. I am at his appointment; the bounds of my habitation are cast in Heaven. No further do I esteem of any mortal man than creatures in his hand. I fear none but the great Jehovah, which hath foretold me of these things, and

I do verily believe that he will deliver me out of your hands. Therefore take heed how you proceed against me, for I know that for this you go about to do to me, God will ruin you and your posterity, and this whole State.

Afterward

The General Court of Massachusetts Bay found Anne Hutchinson guilty of sedition. Her punishment was exile - *Mistress Hutchinson, the sentence of this Court is that you are banished from out of our jurisdiction as being a women not fit for our society.* She was then tried for heresy and found guilty by a Church Court. Her punishment was excommunication - *You are commanded as a leper to withdraw yourself out of this congregation.* Exiled and excommunicated, Anne Hutchinson, finally free to practice her religious beliefs, went on to found religious communities in Rhode Island and the New Netherlands. She was killed in an Indian massacre in August, 1643. There is today a monument to Anne Hutchinson at the Massachusetts State House in Boston. The inscription reads, *Courageous Exponent of Civil Liberty and Religious Toleration.*

Selected Reading

Auger, Helen, *American Jezebel: The Life of Anne Hutchinson,* 1930.

Bremer, Francis J., Editor, *Anne Hutchinson, Troubler of the Puritan Zion,* 1981.

Cameron, Jean. *Anne Hutchinson, Guilty or Not?: A Closer Look at Her Trials,* 1994.

Curtis, Edith R., *Anne Hutchinson: A Biography,* 1930.

Rugg, Winnifred K., *Unafraid: A Life of Anne Hutchinson,* 1970.

Fiction

Heidish, Marcy, *Witnesses: A Novel,* 1980.

John Jay
Address To The People Of England
October 18, 1774

Mr. Jay is a man of wit, a good speaker, and an eloquent writer.
- John Adams (1774)

John Jay is the finest writer in America.
- Thomas Jefferson (1774)

On September 5, 1774, the First Continental Congress met in Philadelphia's Carpenter's Hall to discuss their colonies' response to King George III's arbitrary taxation and continued oppression. On September 17 radical delegates led by Virginia's Patrick Henry proposed separation from England. On September 28 conservative delegates led by Pennsylvania's Joseph Galloway proposed a closer union with England. In the debates that followed, the radical Patrick Henry met his match in New York's moderate John Jay.

John Jay was born on December 12, 1745 in New York City, the son of Peter and Mary (Van Cortlandt) Jay. Educated at Kings College (now Columbia University), he graduated in 1764 and served a four-year legal apprenticeship before being admitted to the bar in 1768. Jay began working for the patriot cause in 1770 as a direct result of the infamous Boston Massacre. As a member of New York's Committee of Correspondence, his tireless work earned him election to the First Continental Congress.

On October 11, 1774, the Continental Congress appointed John Jay to explain America's grievances against King George III to the people of England. Jay's landmark *Address To The People Of England*, as read to the Congress on October 18, 1774, follows.

John Jay

Friends and fellow subjects, when a nation led to greatness by the hand of liberty, and possessed of all the glory that heroism, munificence, and humanity can bestow, descends to the ungrateful task of forging chains for her friends and children, and, instead of giving support to freedom, turns advocate for slavery and oppression, there is reason to suspect she has either ceased to be virtuous or been extremely negligent in the appointment of her rulers.

In almost every age, in repeated conflicts in long and bloody wars, as well civil as foreign, against many and powerful nations, against the open assaults of enemies, and the more dangerous treachery of friends, have the inhabitants of your island, your great and glorious ancestors, maintained their independence and transmitted the rights of men and the blessings of liberty to you, their posterity.

Be not surprised, therefore, that we who are descended from the same common ancestors, that we whose forefathers participated in all the rights, the liberties, and the Constitution you so justly boast of, and who have carefully conveyed the same fair inheritance to us, guaranteed by the plighted faith of Government, and the most solemn compacts with British sovereigns, should refuse to surrender them to men who found their claims on no principles of reason, and who prosecute them with a design that, by having our lives and property in their power, they may, with the greatest facility, enslave you.

The cause of America is now the object of universal attention; it has at length become very serious. This unhappy country has not only been oppressed, but abused and misrepresented; and the duty we owe to ourselves and posterity, to your interest, and the general welfare of the British

Empire, leads us to address you on this very important subject.

Know, then, that we consider ourselves, and do insist, that we are and ought to be as free as our fellow-subjects in Britain, and that no power on earth has a right to take our property from us without our consent.

That we claim all the benefits secured to the subject by the English Constitution, and particularly that inestimable one of trial by jury.

That we hold it essential to English liberty that no man be condemned unheard, or punished for supposed offenses, without having an opportunity of making his defense.

That we think the legislature of Great Britain is not authorized by the Constitution to establish a religion fraught with sanguinary and impious tenets, or to erect an arbitrary form of government in any quarter of the globe. These rights we, as well as you, deem sacred; and yet, sacred as they are, they have, with many others, been repeatedly and flagrantly violated.

Are not the proprietors of the soil of Great Britain lords of their own property? Can it be taken from them without their consent? Will they yield it to the arbitrary disposal of any man or number of men whatever? You know they will not.

Why, then, are the proprietors of the soil of America less lords of their property than you are of yours? or why should they submit it to the disposal of your Parliament, or any other parliament or council in the world, not of their election? Can the intervention of the sea that divides us cause disparity in rights, or can any reason be given why English subjects who live three thousand miles from the royal palace should enjoy less liberty than those who are three hundred miles distant from it?

Reason looks with indignation on such distinctions, and freemen can never perceive their propriety. And yet, however chimerical and unjust such discriminations are, the Parliament assert that they have a right to bind us, in all cases, without exception, whether we consent or not, that they may take and use our property when and in what manner they please, that we are pensioners on their bounty for all that we possess, and can hold it no longer than they vouchsafe to permit. Such declarations we consider as heresies in English politics, and which can no more operate to deprive us of our property than the interdicts of the Pope can divest kings of scepters which the laws of the land and the voice of the people have placed in their hands.

At the conclusion of the late war - a war rendered glorious by the abilities and integrity of a minister to whose efforts the British empire owes its safety and its fame - at the conclusion of this war, which was succeeded by an inglorious peace, formed under the auspices of a minister of principles, and of a family, unfriendly to the Protestant cause, and inimical to liberty - we say at this period, and under the influence of that man, a plan for enslaving your fellow-subjects in America was concerted, and has ever since been pertinaciously carrying into execution.

Prior to this era you were content with drawing from us the wealth produced by our commerce; you restrained your trade in every way that could conduce to your emolument. You exercised unbounded sovereignty over the sea. You named the ports and nations to which alone our merchandise should be carried, and with whom alone we should trade; and though some of these restrictions were grievous, we nevertheless did not complain. We looked up to you as to our parent State, to which we were bound by the strongest ties, and were happy in being instrumental to your prosperity and your grandeur.

We call upon you yourselves to witness our loyalty and attachment to the common interest of the whole empire. Did we not in the last war add all the strength of this vast continent to the force which repelled our common enemy? Did we not leave our native shores and meet disease and death to promote the success of British arms in foreign climates? Did you not thank us for our zeal, and even reimburse us large sums of money, which you confessed we had advanced beyond our proportion, and far beyond our abilities? You did.

To what causes, then, are we to attribute the sudden change of treatment and that system of slavery which was prepared for us at the restoration of peace?

Before we had recovered from the distresses which ever attend war, an attempt was made to drain this country of all its money by the oppressive Stamp Act. Paint, glass, and other commodities, which you would not permit us to purchase of other nations, were taxed; nay, although no wine is made in any country subject to the British State, you prohibited our procuring it of foreigners without paying a tax imposed by your Parliament on all we imported. These, and many other impositions, were laid upon us, most unjustly and unconstitutionally, for the express purpose of raising a revenue. In order to silence complaint, it was indeed provided that this revenue should be expended in America for its protection and defense. These exactions, however, can receive no justification from a pretended necessity of protecting and defending us. They are lavishly squandered on court favorites and ministerial dependents, generally avowed enemies to America, and employing themselves by partial representations to traduce and embroil the Colonies.

For the necessary support of government here, we ever were and ever shall be ready to provide. And whenever the exigencies of the State may require it, we shall, as we have heretofore done, cheerfully contribute our full proportion of men and money. To enforce this unconstitutional and unjust scheme of taxation, every fence that the wisdom of our British ancestors had carefully erected against arbitrary power has been violently thrown down in America, and the inestimable right of trial by jury taken away in cases that touch both life and property. . . .

By the course of our law, offenses committed in such of the British dominions in which courts are established, and justice duly and regularly administered, shall be there tried by a jury of the vicinage. There the offenders and the witnesses are known, and the degree of credibility to be given to their testimony can be ascertained.

In all these Colonies justice is regularly and impartially administered; and yet, by the construction of some, and the direction of other acts of Parliament, offenders are to be taken by force, together with all such persons as may be pointed out as witnesses, and carried to England, there to be tried in a distant land by a jury of strangers, and subject to all the disadvantages that result from the want of friends, want of witnesses, and want of money.

When the design of raising a revenue from the duties imposed on the importation of tea into America had in great measure been rendered abortive by our ceasing to import that commodity, a scheme was concerted by the ministry with the East India Company, and an act passed, enabling and encouraging them to transport and vend it in the

Colonies. Aware of the danger of giving success to this insidious maneuver, and of permitting a precedent of taxation thus to be established among us, various methods were adopted to elude the stroke. The people of Boston, then ruled by a governor whom, as well as his predecessor, Sir Francis Bernard, all America considers as her enemy, were exceedingly embarrassed. The ships which had arrived with the tea were, by his management, prevented from returning. The duties would have been paid; the cargoes landed and exposed to sale; a governor's influence would have procured and protected many purchasers. While the town was suspended by deliberations on this important subject, the tea was destroyed. Even supposing a trespass was thereby committed, and the proprietors of the tea entitled to·damages, the courts of law were open, and judges, appointed by the Crown, presided in them. The East India Company, however, did not think proper to commence any suits, nor did they even demand satisfaction, either from individuals or from the community in general. The ministry, it seems, officiously made the case their own, and the great council of the nation descended to intermeddle with a dispute about private property. Diverse papers, letters, and other unauthenticated ex parte evidence were laid before them. Neither the persons who destroyed the tea, nor the people of Boston, were called upon to answer the complaint. The ministry, incensed by being disappointed in a favorite scheme, were determined to recur from the little arts of finesse to open force and unmanly violence. The port of Boston was blocked up by a fleet, and an army placed in the town. Their trade was to be suspended, and thousands reduced to the necessity of gaining subsistence from charity, till they should submit to pass under the yoke and consent to become slaves, by confessing the omnipotence of Parliament, and acquiescing in whatever disposition they might think proper to make of their lives and property.

Let justice and humanity cease to be the boast of your nation! Consult your history; examine your records of former transactions; nay, turn to the annals of the many arbitrary states and kingdoms that surround you, and show us a single instance of men being condemned to suffer for imputed crimes, unheard, unquestioned, and without even the specious formality of a trial, and that, too, by laws made expressly for the purpose, and which had no existence at the time of the act committed. If it be difficult to reconcile these proceedings to the genius and temper of your laws and Constitution, the task will become more arduous when we call upon our ministerial enemies to justify not only condemning men untried and by hearsay, but involving the innocent in one common punishment with the guilty, and for the act of thirty or forty to bring poverty, distress, and calamity on thirty thousand souls and those not your enemies, but your friends, brethren, and fellow-subjects.

It would be some consolation to us if the catalog of American oppressions ended here. It gives us pain to be reduced to the necessity of reminding you that under the confidence reposed in the faith of Government, pledged in a royal charter from a British sovereign, the forefathers of the present inhabitants of the Massachusetts Bay left their former habitations, and established that great, flourishing, and loyal Colony. Without incurring or being charged with a forfeiture of their rights, without being heard, without being tried, without law and without justice, by an act of Parliament their charter is destroyed, their liberties violated, their Constitution and form of government changed, and all this upon no better pretense than because in one of their towns a trespass was committed on some merchandise, said to belong to one of the companies, and because the ministry were of opinion that such high political regulations were necessary to compel due subordination and obedience to their mandates.

Nor are these the only capital grievances under which we labor. We might tell of dissolute, weak, and wicked governors having been set over us, of legislatures being suspended for asserting the rights of British subjects, of needy and ignorant dependents on great men advanced to the seats of justice, and to other places of trust and importance, of hard restrictions on commerce, and a great variety of lesser evils, the recollection of which is almost lost under the weight and pressure of greater and more poignant calamities.

Now mark the progression of the ministerial plan for enslaving us.

Well aware that such hardy attempts to take our property from us, to deprive us of that valuable right of trial by jury, to seize our persons, and carry us for trial to Great Britain, to blockade our ports, to destroy our charters and change our forms of government, would occasion, and had already occasioned, great discontent in the Colonies (which might produce opposition to these measures), an act was passed to protect, indemnify, and screen from punishment such as might be guilty even of murder, in endeavoring to carry their oppressive edicts into execution. And by another act, the Dominion of Canada is to be so extended, modeled, and governed as that, by being disunited from us, detached from our interests, by civil as well as religious prejudices, that by their numbers daily swelling with Catholic emigrants from Europe, and by their devotion to an administration so friendly to their religion, they might become formidable to us, and on occasion be fit instruments, in the hands of power, to reduce the ancient free Protestant Colonies to the same state of slavery with themselves.

This was evidently the object of the act; and in this view, being extremely dangerous to our liberty and quiet, we cannot forbear complaining of it as hostile to British America. Superadded to these considerations, we cannot help deploring the unhappy condition to which it has reduced the many English settlers who, encouraged by the royal proclamation, promising the enjoyment of all their rights, have purchased estates in that country. They are now the subjects of an arbitrary government, deprived of trial by jury, and when imprisoned cannot claim the benefit of the Habeas Corpus Act - that great bulwark and palladium of English liberty. Nor can we suppress our astonishment that a British Parliament should ever consent to establish in that country a religion that has deluged your island in blood and dispersed impiety, bigotry, persecution, murder, and rebellion through every part of the world.

This being a true state of facts, let us beseech you to consider to what end they may lead.

Admit that the ministry, by the powers of Britain and the aid of our Roman Catholic neighbors, should be able to carry the point of taxation, and reduce us to a state of perfect humiliation and slavery. Such an enterprise would doubtless make some addition to your national debt, which already presses down your liberties and fills you with pensioners and placemen. We presume, also, that your commerce will be somewhat diminished. However, suppose you should prove victorious, in what condition will you then be? What advantages or laurels will you reap from such a conquest?

May not a ministry with the same armies enslave you? It may be said, you will cease to pay them - but remember the taxes from America, the wealth, and we may add the men, and particularly the Roman Catholics of this vast continent will then be in the power of your enemies; nor will you have any reason to expect that after making slaves of us, many among us should refuse to assist in reducing you to the same abject state.

Do not treat this as chimerical. Know that in less than half a century the quit rents reserved to the Crown, from the numberless grants of this vast continent, will pour large streams of wealth into the royal coffers, and if to this be added the power of taxing America at pleasure, the Crown will be rendered independent of you for supplies and will possess more treasure than may be necessary to purchase the remains of liberty in your island. In a word, take care that you do not fall into the pit that is preparing for us.

We believe there is yet much virtue, much justice, and much public spirit in the English nation. To that justice we now appeal. You have been told that we are seditious, impatient of government, and desirous of independence. Be assured that these are not facts, but calumnies. Permit us to be as free as yourselves, and we shall ever esteem a union with you to be our greatest glory, and our greatest happiness; we shall ever be ready to contribute all in our power to the welfare of the empire; we shall consider your enemies as our enemies, and your interest as our own.

But if you are determined that your ministers shall wantonly sport with the rights of mankind - if neither the voice of justice, the dictates of the law, the principles of the Constitution, nor the suggestions of humanity can restrain your hands from shedding human blood in such an impious cause - we must then tell you that we will never submit to be hewers of wood or drawers of water for any ministry or nation in the world.

Place us in the same situation that we were in at the close of the last war, and our former harmony will be restored.

But lest the same supineness and the same inattention to our common interest which you have for several years shown should continue, we think it prudent to anticipate the consequences.

By the destruction of the trade of Boston, the ministry have endeavored to induce submission to their measures. The like fate may befall us all. We will endeavor, therefore, to live without trade, and recur for subsistence to the fertility and bounty of our native soil, which will afford us all the necessaries and some of the conveniences of life. We have suspended our importation from Great Britain and Ireland, and, in less than a year's time, unless our grievances should be redressed, shall discontinue our exports to those kingdoms and the West Indies.

It is with the utmost regret, however, that we find ourselves compelled, by the overruling principles of self-preservation, to adopt measures detrimental in their consequences to numbers of our fellow-subjects in Great Britain and Ireland. But we hope that the magnanimity and justice of the British nation will furnish a Parliament of such wisdom, independence, and public spirit as may save the violated rights of the whole empire from the devices of wicked ministers and evil counselors, whether in or out of office, and thereby restore that harmony, friendship, and fraternal affection between all the inhabitants of his Majesty's kingdoms and territories so ardently wished for by every true and honest American.

John Jay

Afterward

When the War of American Independence began on the morning of April 19, 1775, John Jay's *measure of arbitrary power* was at last full. Jay continued to serve as a New York delegate to the Continental Congress, where he was elected its President. As a proponent of the Constitution, he co-authored (with James Madison and Alexander Hamilton) *The Federalist Papers.* Jay served in diplomatic posts as Ambassador to Spain, as peace negotiator (with Benjamin Franklin and John Adams) with Great Britain, as President Washington's Minister of Foreign Affairs, as Chief Justice of the U.S. Supreme Court, and as Governor of the State of New York.

John Jay retired from public life in 1795 and died in Westchester County, New York on May 17, 1829.

Selected Reading

Jay, William, *The Life of John Jay,* 1972.

Johnston, Henry P., Editor, *The Correspondence and Public Papers of John Jay,* 1970.

Morris, Richard B., Editor, *John Jay: The Making of a Revolutionary,* 1975.

————, *Witness at the Creation,* 1985.

Pellew, George, *John Jay,* 1890.

Smith, Donald L., *John Jay: Founder of a State and Nation,* 1968.

Whitelock, William, *The Life and Times of John Jay,* 1887.

Thomas Jefferson
The First Public Readings Of
The Declaration Of Independence
July 8-9, 1776

The Declaration of Independence] was intended to be an expression of the American mind, and to give to that expression the proper tone and spirit called for by the occasion. **- Thomas Jefferson (1825)**

Thomas Jefferson was born at *Shadwell* Plantation in Goochland (now Albemarle) County, Virginia on April 13, 1743, the son of Peter and Jane (Randolph) Jefferson. On August 17, 1757, upon the death of his father, Thomas Jefferson, age fourteen, inherited the thousand acre plantation and its slaves. Jefferson spent two years at the College of William and Mary and studied the law for five years. In 1764 he had assumed to the management of *Shadwell* Plantation and in 1769 he began the building of a second plantation, *Monticello.* Elected six times to Virginia's House of Burgesses, Thomas Jefferson came to national fame in 1774 upon the publication of *A Summary View of the Rights of British America.* He was selected by the Virginia Convention to serve as a delegate to the Second Continental Congress. Jefferson arrived in Philadelphia on May 14, 1776.

On June 11, 1776, Thomas Jefferson was appointed to a Committee selected to draft a Declaration of Independence. On June 28 he submitted his first draft to the Committee. John Adams and Benjamin Franklin, in consultation with Jefferson, then made deletions and additions. The edited draft was submitted to and debated by the Continental Congress on July 1-3. On July 4, 1776, the delegates of the thirteen colonies voted for its adoption. The Declaration of Independence was read for the first time to the general public in Philadelphia on July 8, 1776 and to the Continental Army in New York City on July 9, 1776.

Thomas Jefferson

A Declaration by the Representatives of the United States of America, in General Congress assembled:

When, in the course of human events, it becomes necessary for one people to dissolve the political bands which have connected them with another, and to assume among the powers of the earth the separate and equal station to which the laws of nature and of nature's God entitle them, a decent respect to the opinions of mankind requires that they should declare the causes which impel them to the separation.

We hold these truths to be self-evident - that all men are created equal, that they are endowed by their Creator with certain unalienable rights, that among these are life, liberty, and the pursuit of happiness, that to secure these rights, governments are instituted among men, deriving their just powers from the consent of the governed, that whenever any form of government becomes destructive of these ends, it is the right of the people to alter or to abolish it, and to institute new government, laying its foundation on such principles, and organizing its powers in such form as to them shall seem most likely to effect their safety and happiness. Prudence, indeed, will dictate that governments long established should not be changed for light and transient causes, and accordingly all experience hath shown that mankind are more disposed to suffer while evils are sufferable than to right themselves by abolishing the forms to which they are accustomed. But when a long train of abuses and usurpations pursuing invariably the same object evinces a design to reduce them under absolute despotism, it is their right, it is their duty to throw off such government, and to provide new guards for their future security. Such has been the patient sufferance of these colonies; and such is now the necessity which constrains them to alter their former systems of government. The history of the present King of Great Britain is a history of repeated injuries and usurpations, all having in direct object the establishment of an absolute tyranny over these States.

To prove this, let facts be submitted to a candid world.

He has refused his assent to laws the most wholesome and necessary for the public good.

He has forbidden his governors to pass laws of immediate and pressing importance, unless suspended in their operation till his assent should be obtained; and, when so suspended, he has utterly neglected to attend to them.

He has refused to pass other laws for the accommodation of large districts of people, unless those people would relinquish the right of representation in the Legislature, a right inestimable to them, and formidable to tyrants only.

He has called together legislative bodies at places unusual, uncomfortable, and distant from the depository of their public records, for the sole purpose of fatiguing them into compliance with his measures.

He has dissolved representative houses repeatedly for opposing with manly firmness his invasions on the rights of the people.

He has refused for a long time after such dissolutions to cause others to be elected, whereby the legislative powers, incapable of annihilation, have returned to the people at large for their exercise, the State remaining, in the meantime, exposed to all the dangers of invasion from without and convulsions within.

He has endeavored to prevent the population of these States, for that purpose obstructing the laws for naturalization of foreigners, refusing to pass others to encourage their migrations hither, and raising the conditions of new appropriations of lands.

He has obstructed the administration of justice by refusing his assent to laws for establishing judiciary powers.

He has made judges dependent on his will alone for the tenure of their offices, and the amount and payment of their salaries.

He has erected a multitude of new offices and sent hither swarms of officers to harass our people and eat out their substance.

He has kept among us in times of peace standing armies, without the consent of our Legislatures.

He has effected to render the military independent of, and superior to, the civil power.

He has combined with others to subject us to a jurisdiction foreign to our constitution and unacknowledged by our laws, giving his assent to their acts of pretended legislation - for quartering large bodies of armed troops among us, for protecting them by a mock trial from punishment for any murders which they should commit on the inhabitants of these States, for cutting off our trade with all parts of the world, for imposing taxes on us without our consent, for depriving us in many cases of the benefits of trial by jury, for transporting us beyond seas to be tried for pretended offenses, for abolishing the free system of English laws in a neighboring province, establishing therein an arbitrary government and enlarging its boundaries so as to render it at once an example and fit instrument for introducing the same absolute rule into these Colonies, for taking away our charters, abolishing our most valuable laws, and altering fundamentally the forms of our governments, for suspending our own Legislatures and declaring themselves invested with power to legislate for us in all cases whatsoever.

He has abdicated government here by declaring us out of his protection and waging war against us.

He has plundered our seas, ravaged our coasts, burnt our towns, and destroyed the lives of our people.

He is at this time transporting large armies of foreign mercenaries to complete the work of death, desolation, and tyranny already begun with circumstances of cruelty and perfidy scarcely paralleled in the most barbarous ages and totally unworthy the head of a civilized nation.

He has constrained our fellow-citizens taken captive on the high seas to bear arms against their country, to become the executioners of their friends and brethren, or to fall themselves by their hands.

He has excited domestic insurrections amongst us, and has endeavored to bring on the inhabitants of our frontiers, the merciless Indian savages, whose known rule of warfare is an undistinguished destruction of all ages, sexes, and conditions.

In every stage of these oppressions we have petitioned for redress in the most humble terms; our repeated petitions have been answered only by repeated injury.

A prince whose character is thus marked by every act which may define a tyrant is unfit to be the ruler of a free people.

Nor have we been wanting in attentions to our British brethren. We have warned them from time to time of attempts by their legislature to extend an unwarrantable jurisdiction over us. We have reminded them of the circumstances of our emigration and settlement here. We have appealed to their native justice and magnanimity, and we have conjured them by the ties of our common kindred to disavow these usurpations, which would inevitably interrupt our connections and correspondence. They, too, have been deaf to the voice of justice and of consanguinity. We must therefore acquiesce in the necessity, which denounces our separation, and hold them, as we hold the rest of mankind, enemies in war, in peace, friends.

We, therefore, the representatives of the United States of America, in General Congress assembled, appealing to the Supreme Judge of the world, for the rectitude of our intention, do, in the name, and by authority of the good people of these Colonies, solemnly publish and declare that these united Colonies are, and of right ought to be, free and independent States, that they are absolved from all allegiance to the British Crown, and that all political connection between them and the State of Great Britain is and ought to be totally dissolved, and that, as free and independent States, they have full power to levy war, conclude peace, contract alliances, establish commerce, and to do all other acts and things which independent States may of right do.

And for the support of this Declaration, with a firm reliance on the protection of divine Providence, we mutually pledge to each other our lives, our fortunes, and our sacred honor.

Afterward

Thomas Jefferson, author of the Declaration of Independence, went on to serve as Governor of Virginia, Minister to France, President Washington's Secretary of State, President Adams' Vice President, President of the United States, and thereafter as Rector of the University of Virginia. Jefferson died on July 4, 1826, the 50th anniversary of the Declaration of Independence. His last words were reported to have been, *Is this the Fourth?*

Selected Reading

Commager, Henry S., *Jefferson, Nationalism, and the Enlightenment*, 1975.

Harrison, Maureen, and Steve Gilbert, Editors, *Thomas Jefferson: Word for Word*, 1993.

Malone, Dumas, *Jefferson And His Time*, 1982.

Randall, Willard, *Thomas Jefferson: A Life*, 1993.

Schachner, Nathan, *Thomas Jefferson: A Biography*, 1957.

Henry Lee
The Death Of George Washington
December 26, 1799

The fame and memory of George Washington was the fondly cherished passion to which Henry Lee clung amid the wreck of his fortunes - the hope, which gave warmth to his heart when all else around him seemed cold and desolate. **- George Washington Parke Curtis,**
Recollections of Washington

Henry Lee was born on January 29, 1756 at the family plantation, *Leesylvania*, in Prince William County, Virginia. He was the son of Henry and Lucy (Grymes) Lee. Educated at the College of New Jersey (now Princeton University), Lee graduated in 1773. In 1776 he volunteered his services to Virginia and was appointed a Captain in the Cavalry. In 1777 his regiment joined General Washington's Continental Army, where the two, during the long winter in Valley Forge, began a close, lifelong friendship. Henry Lee rose to the rank of Major and was given the command of a mixed cavalry and infantry unit that carried the name of *Lee's Legion*. On July 19, 1779, at the Battle of Paulus Hook, New Jersey, Lee won a brilliant victory, capturing, without suffering any casualties, a British fort. *Light Horse Harry* went on to be one of the leading military figures of the Revolutionary War.

In the post-War period, Henry Lee served terms in the Virginia Assembly and as Virginia Governor. He also served in the Continental and United States Congress. He returned to active service when President Washington called him to lead the Army in quelling the 1794 Whiskey Rebellion.

George Washington died on December 14, 1799. Henry Lee was selected by Congress to write this landmark *Eulogy For Washington*, which he delivered in Philadelphia on December 26, 1799.

In obedience to your will, I rise your humble organ, with the hope of executing a part of the system of public mourning which you have been pleased to adopt, commemorative of the death of the most illustrious and most beloved personage this country has ever produced. . . .

Desperate, indeed, is any attempt on earth to meet correspondently this dispensation of Heaven, for, while with pious resignation we submit to the will of an all-gracious Providence, we can never cease lamenting, in our finite view of Omnipotent Wisdom, the heart-rending privation for which our nation weeps. When the civilized world shakes to its center, when every moment gives birth to strange and momentous changes, when our peaceful quarter of the globe - exempt as it happily has been from any share in the slaughter of the human race - may yet be compelled to abandon her pacific policy, and to risk the doleful casualties of war, what limit is there to the extent of our loss? None within the reach of my words to express, none which your feelings will not disavow.

The founder of our federate republic, our bulwark in war, our guide in peace, is no more! O that this were but questionable! Hope, the comforter of the wretched, would pour into our agonizing hearts its balmy dew. But alas! there is no hope for us; our Washington is removed forever! Possessing the stoutest frame and purest mind, he had passed nearly to his sixty-eighth year, in the enjoyment of high health, when, habituated by his care of us to neglect himself, a slight cold disregarded became inconvenient on Friday, oppressive on Saturday, and, defying every medical interposition, before the morning of Sunday, put an end to the best of men. An end, did I say? His fame survives, bounded only by the limits of the earth and by the extent of the human mind. He survives in our hearts, in the growing knowledge of our children, in the affection of the good throughout the world. And when our monuments shall be done away, when nations now existing shall be no more, when even our young and far-spreading empire shall have perished, still will our Washington's glory unfaded shine, and die not until the love of virtue cease on earth, or earth itself sink into chaos.

How, my fellow-citizens, shall I single to your grateful hearts his preeminent worth? When shall I begin in opening to your view a character throughout sublime? Shall I speak of his warlike achievements, all springing from obedience to his country's will, all directed to his country's good?

Will you go with me to the banks of the Monongahela to see your youthful Washington supporting in the dismal hour of Indian victory the ill-fated Braddock, and saving, by his judgment and by his valor, the remains of a defeated army, pressed by the conquering savage foe? or when, oppressed, America nobly resolving to risk her all, in defense of her violated rights, he was elevated by the unanimous voice of Congress to the command of her armies? Will you follow him to the high grounds of Boston, where to an undisciplined, courageous, and virtuous yeomanry, his presence gave the stability of system, and infused the invincibility of love of country? Or shall I carry you to the painful scenes of Long Island, York Island, and New Jersey, when, combating superior and gallant armies, aided by powerful fleets, and led by chiefs high in the roll of fame, he stood the bulwark of our safety, undismayed by disaster, unchanged by change of fortune? Or will you view him in the precarious fields of Trenton, where deep gloom, unnerving every arm, reigned triumphant through our thinned, worn down, unaided ranks - himself unmoved? Dreadful was the night. It was about this time of winter. The storm raged.

The Delaware, rolling furiously with floating ice, forbade the approach of man. Washington, self-collected, viewed the tremendous scene. His country called. Unappalled by surrounding dangers, he passed the hostile shore; he fought; he conquered. The morning sun cheered the American world. Our country rose on the event; and her dauntless chief, pursuing his blow, completed in the lawns of Princeton what his vast soul had conceived on the shores of Delaware.

Thence to the strong grounds of Morristown he led his small but gallant band; and through an eventful winter, by the high efforts of his genius, whose matchless force was measurable only by the growth of difficulties, he held in check formidable hostile legions, conducted by a chief experienced in the art of war, and famed for his valor on the ever-memorable Height of Abraham, where fell Wolfe, Montcalm, and, since, our much-lamented Montgomery - all covered with glory. In this fortunate interval produced by his masterly conduct, our fathers, ourselves, animated by his resistless example, rallied around our country's standard, and continued to follow her beloved chief through the various and trying scenes to which the destinies of our Union led.

Who is there that has forgotten the vales of Brandywine, the fields of Germantown, or the plains of Monmouth? Everywhere present, wants of every kind obstructing, numerous and valiant armies encountering, himself a host, he assuaged our sufferings, limited our privations, and upheld our tottering republic. Shall I display to you the spread of the fire of his soul by rehearsing the praises of the hero of Saratoga and his much-loved compeer of the Carolinas? No; our Washington needs not borrowed glory. To Gates, to Greene, he gave without reserve the applause due to their eminent merit; and long may the chiefs of Saratoga and of Eutaw receive the grateful respect of a grateful people.

Moving in his own orbit, he imparted heat and light to his most distant satellites; and combining the physical and moral force of all within his sphere, with irresistible weight he took his course, commiserating folly, disdaining vice, dismaying treason, and invigorating despondency - until the auspicious hour arrived, when, united with the intrepid forces of a potent and magnanimous ally, he brought to submission the since conqueror of India, thus finishing his long career of military glory with a luster corresponding to his great name, and in this his last act of war affixing the seal of fate to our nation's birth.

To the horrid din of battle, sweet peace succeeded; and our virtuous chief, mindful only of the common good, in a moment tempting personal aggrandizement, hushed the discontents of growing sedition, and, surrendering his power into the hands from which he had received it, converted his sword into a ploughshare, teaching an admiring world that to be truly great you must be truly good.

Were I to stop here, the picture would be incomplete, and the task imposed unfinished. Great as was our Washington in war, and as much as did that greatness contribute to produce the American republic, it is not in war alone that his preeminence stands conspicuous. His various talents, combining all the capacities of a statesman with those of a soldier, fitted him alike to guide the councils and the armies of our nation. Scarcely had he rested from his martial toils, while his invaluable parental advice was still sounding in our ears, when he, who had been our shield and our sword, was called forth to act a less splendid, but more important, part.

Possessing a clear and penetrating mind, a strong and sound judgment, calmness and temper for deliberation, with invincible firmness and perseverance in resolutions maturely formed, drawing information from all, acting from himself with incorruptible integrity and unvarying patriotism, his own superiority and the public confidence alike marked him as the man designed by Heaven to lead in the great political as well as military events which have distinguished the era of his life.

The finger of an overruling Providence, pointing at Washington, was neither mistaken nor unobserved, when, to realize the vast hopes to which our revolution had given birth, a change of political system became indispensable.

How novel, how grand the spectacle! Independent States stretched over an immense territory, and known only by common difficulty, clinging to their union as the rock of their safety, deciding, by frank comparison of their relative condition, to rear on that rock, under the guidance of reason, a common government, through whose commanding protection, liberty and order, with their long train of blessings, should be safe to themselves, and the sure inheritance of their posterity.

. . . . To have framed a Constitution was showing only, without realizing, the general happiness. This great work remained to be done; and America, steadfast in her preference, with one voice summoned her beloved Washington, unpracticed as he was in the duties of civil administration, to execute this last act in the completion of the national felicity. Obedient to her call, he assumed the high office with that self-distrust peculiar to his innate modesty, the constant attendant of preeminent virtue. What was the burst of joy through our anxious land on this exhilarating event is known to us all. . . .

Commencing his administration, what heart is not charmed with the recollection of the pure and wise principles announced by himself as the basis of his political life? He best understood the indissoluble union between virtue and happiness, between duty and advantage, between the genuine maxims of an honest and magnanimous policy and the solid rewards of public prosperity and individual felicity. Watching with an equal and comprehensive eye over this great assemblage of communities and interests, he laid the foundations of our national policy in the unerring, immutable principles of morality, based on religion, exemplifying the preeminence of a free government by all the attributes which win the affections of its citizens, or command the respect of the world. . . .

Leading through the complicated difficulties produced by previous obligations and conflicting interests, seconded by succeeding Houses of Congress, enlightened and patriotic, he surmounted all original obstruction and brightened the path of our national felicity.

The presidential term expiring, his solicitude to exchange exaltation for humility returned with a force increased with increase of age; and he had prepared his Farewell Address to his countrymen, proclaiming his intention, when the united interposition of all around him, enforced by the eventful prospects of the epoch, produced a further sacrifice of inclination to duty. The election of President followed; and Washington was, by the unanimous vote of the nation, called to resume the chief magistracy. What a wonderful fixture of confidence! Which attracts most our admiration, a people so correct, or a citizen combining an assemblage of talents forbidding rivalry, and stifling even envy itself? Such a nation ought to be happy; such a chief must be forever revered.

War, long menaced by the Indian tribes, now broke out; and the terrible conflict, deluging Europe with blood, began to shed its baneful influence over our happy land. To the first, outstretching his invincible arm, under the orders of the gallant Wayne, the American eagle soared triumphant through distant forests. Peace followed victory, and the melioration of the condition of the enemy followed peace. Godlike virtue! which uplifts even the subdued savage.

To the second he opposed himself. New and delicate was the juncture, and great was the stake. Soon did his penetrating mind discern and seize the only course, continuing to us all the felicity enjoyed. He issued his proclamation of neutrality. This index to his whole subsequent conduct was sanctioned by the approbation of both Houses of Congress, and by the approving voice of the people.

To this sublime policy he inviolably adhered, unmoved by foreign intrusion, unshaken by domestic turbulence. . . .

Maintaining his pacific system at the expense of no duty, America, faithful to herself, and unstained in her honor, continued to enjoy the delights of peace, while afflicted Europe mourns in every quarter, under the accumulated miseries of an unexampled war - miseries in which our happy country must have shared had not our preeminent Washington been as firm in council as he was brave in the field.

Pursuing steadfastly his course, he held safe the public happiness, preventing foreign war, and quelling internal discord, till the revolving period of a third election approached, when he executed his interrupted, but inextinguishable desire of returning to the humble walks of private life.

The promulgation of his fixed resolution stopped the anxious wishes of an affectionate people from adding a third unanimous testimonial of their unabated confidence in the man so long enthroned in their hearts. Where before was affection like this exhibited on earth? Turn over the records of ancient Greece, review the annals of mighty Rome, examine the volumes of modern Europe - you search in vain. America and her Washington alone afford the dignified exemplification.

The illustrious personage, called by the national voice in succession to the arduous office of guiding a free people, had new difficulties to encounter. The amicable effort of settling our difficulties with France, begun by Washington (and pursued by his successor in virtue as in station) proving abortive, America took measures for self-defense. No sooner was the public mind roused by a prospect of danger than every eye was turned to the friend of all, though secluded from public view, and gray in public service. The virtuous veteran, following his plough, received the unexpected summons with mingled emotions of indignation at the unmerited ill-treatment of his country and of a determination once more to risk his all in her defense. The annunciation of these feelings in his affecting letter to the President, accepting the command of the army, concludes his official conduct.

First in war, first in peace, and first in the hearts of his countrymen, he was second to none in the humble and endearing scenes of private life. Pious, just, humane, temperate, sincere, uniform, dignified, and commanding, his example was as edifying to all around him as were the effects of that example lasting.

To his equals he was condescending, to his inferiors kind, and to the dear object of his affections exemplary tender. Correct throughout, vice shudders in his presence, and virtue always felt his fostering hand. The purity of his private character gave effulgence to his public virtues.

His last scene comported with the tenor of his life. Although in extreme pain, not a sigh, not a groan escaped him; and with undisturbed serenity he closed his well-spent life. Such was the man America has lost! Such was the man for whom our nation mourns!

Methinks I see his august image, and hear, falling from his venerable lips, these deep-sinking words,

> *Cease, sons of America, to mourn our separation. Go on, and confirm by your wisdom the fruits of our joint councils, joint efforts, and common dangers. Reverence religion; diffuse knowledge throughout your land; patronize the arts and sciences; let liberty and order be inseparable companions; control party spirit, the bane of a free government; observe good faith to, and cultivate peace with, all nations; shut up every avenue to foreign influence; contract rather than extend national connection; rely on yourselves only; be American in thought and deed. Thus will you give immortality to that union which was the constant object of my terrestrial labors; thus will you preserve undisturbed to the latest posterity the felicity of a people to me most dear; and thus will you supply (if my happiness is now aught to you) the only vacancy in the round of pure bliss high Heaven bestows.*

Afterward

In 1794 Henry Lee summed up his philosophy of life, *Next to our duty to God is our duty to country, which we completely discharge when to the character of the citizen faithful and obedient to the Constitution and the law, we unite the character of a soldier, ready and determined to vindicate and maintain the dignity and rights of our society.*

Henry Lee, a brilliant General, politician, and orator, was a very poor businessman. In and out of bankruptcy for most of his life, Lee was thrown into jail for non-payment of his debts in 1808-1809. There he wrote his two-volume *Memoirs of the War*, which was published in 1812. An opponent of the policies that led to the War of 1812, Lee was beaten by a mob in Baltimore and never recovered his health. Henry Lee died in poverty and obscurity on Cumberland Island, Georgia on November 25, 1818.

He was the father of Confederate General Robert E. Lee.

Selected Reading
Boyd, Thomas, *Light-Horse Harry Lee*, 1931.

Gerson, Noel B., *Light-Horse Harry: A Biography of Washington's Great Cavalryman, General Henry Lee*, 1966.

Morse, John Torrey, *Memoir of Colonel Henry Lee, With Selections From His Writings and Speeches*, 1905.

Royster, Charles, *Light-Horse Harry Lee*, 1981.

_____, Editor, *The Revolutionary War Memoirs of General Henry Lee*, 1998.

James Madison
American Government
June 6, 1788

The happy Union of these States is a wonder, their Constitution a miracle, their example the hope of liberty throughout the world.
- James Madison (1829)

James Madison, Jr. was born on March 16, 1751 on his family's tobacco plantation, Montpelier, near Port Royal, Virginia. He was the son of James and Eleanor *Nelly* (Conway) Madison. He was educated at the College of New Jersey (now Princeton University). In 1776 he was elected to the Virginia Convention, which was to draft a State Constitution. In 1777 Madison was elected to the Governor's Council and served Virginia's first two governors, Patrick Henry and Thomas Jefferson. In 1779 he was elected to the Second Continental Congress. In 1786 the Second Continental Congress called for a Convention. The Convention began on May 14 and debated until September 17, 1787, when a Federal Constitution was agreed upon. Madison signed it and returned home to work for its ratification.

Madison, along with Alexander Hamilton and John Jay, published *The Federalist Papers* - eighty-five political essays outlining reasons why the ratification of the Constitution was vital to the United States.

Virginia's Constitutional Ratification Convention began debate in Richmond on June 2, 1788. Eight states had ratified the Constitution. Nine were needed for adoption. Madison debated day after day, offering persuasive arguments for ratification.

On June 6 James Madison, ill from weeks of tireless effort and at the point of exhaustion, rose to deliver this landmark speech in clear and logical terms and in quiet and unemotional style.

Mr. Chairman, in what I am about to offer to this assembly, I shall not attempt to make impressions by any ardent professions of zeal for the public welfare. We know that the principles of every man will be, and ought to be, judged not by his professions and declarations, but by his conduct. By that criterion, I wish, in common with every other member, to be judged; and even though it should prove unfavorable to my reputation, yet it is a criterion from which I by no means would depart, nor could if I would. Comparisons have been made between the friends of this Constitution and those who oppose it. Although I disapprove of such comparisons, I trust that in everything that regards truth, honor, candor, and rectitude of motives, the friends of this system, here and in other States, are not inferior to its opponents. But professions of attachment to the public good, and comparisons of parties, at all times invidious, ought not to govern or influence us now. We ought, sir, to examine the Constitution exclusively on its own merits. We ought to inquire whether it will promote the public happiness; and its aptitude to produce that desirable object ought to be the exclusive subject of our researches. . . .

Before I proceed to make some additions to the reasons which have been adduced by my honorable friend over the way, I must take the liberty to make some observations on what was said by another gentleman (Patrick Henry). He told us that this Constitution ought to be rejected, because, in his opinion, it endangered the public liberty in many instances. Give me leave to make one answer to that observation - let the dangers with which this system is supposed to be replete be clearly pointed out. If any dangerous and unnecessary powers be given to the general legislature, let them be plainly demonstrated, and let us not rest satisfied with general assertions of dangers, without proof, without examination. If powers be necessary, apparent danger is not a sufficient reason against conceding them. He has suggested that licentiousness has seldom produced the loss of liberty, but that the tyranny of rulers has almost always effected it. Since the general civilization of mankind, I believe there are more instances of the abridgment of the freedom of the people by gradual and silent encroachments of those in power, than by violent and sudden usurpations; but on a candid examination of history, we shall find that turbulence, violence, and abuse of power, by the majority trampling on the rights of the minority, have produced factions and commotions which, in republics, have, more frequently than any other cause, produced despotism.

If we go over the whole history of ancient and modern republics, we shall find their destruction to have generally resulted from those causes. If we consider the peculiar situation of the United States, and go to the sources of that diversity of sentiment which pervades its inhabitants, we shall find great danger to fear that the same causes may terminate here in the same fatal effects which they produced in those republics. This danger ought to be wisely guarded against. In the progress of this discussion, it will perhaps appear that the only possible remedy for those evils, and the only certain means of preserving and protecting the principles of republicanism, will be found in that very system which is now exclaimed against as the parent of oppression.

I must confess that I have not been able to find his usual consistency in the gentleman's arguments on this occasion. He informs us that the people of this country are at perfect repose, that every man enjoys the fruits of his labor peaceably and securely, and that everything is in perfect tranquillity and safety. I wish sincerely, sir, this were true.

But if this be really their situation, why has every State acknowledged the contrary? Why were deputies from all the States sent to the general convention? Why have complaints of national and individual distresses been echoed and reechoed throughout the continent? Why has our general government been so shamefully disgraced, and our Constitution violated? Wherefore have laws been made to authorize a change, and wherefore are we now assembled here?

A federal government is formed for the protection of its individual members. Ours was itself attacked with impunity. Its authority has been boldly disobeyed and openly despised.

I think I perceive a glaring inconsistency in another of his arguments. He complains of this Constitution, because it requires the consent of at least three-fourths of the States to introduce amendments which shall be necessary for the happiness of the people. The assent of so many he considers as too great an obstacle to the admission of salutary amendments, which he strongly insists ought to be at the will of a bare majority, and we hear this argument at the very moment we are called upon to assign reasons for proposing a Constitution which puts it in the power of nine States to abolish the present inadequate, unsafe, and pernicious confederation! In the first case, he asserts that a majority ought to have the power of altering the government, when found to be inadequate to the security of public happiness. In the last case, he affirms that even three-fourths of the community have not a right to alter a government which experience has proved to be subversive of national felicity; nay, that the most necessary and urgent alterations cannot be made without the absolute unanimity of all the States. Does not the thirteenth Article of the Confederation expressly require that no alteration shall be made without the unanimous consent of all the States? Can anything in theory be more perniciously improvident and injudicious than this submission of the will of the majority to the most trifling minority? Have not experience and practice actually manifested this theoretical inconvenience to be extremely impolitic?

Let me mention one fact, which I conceive must carry conviction to the mind of anyone - the smallest State in the Union has obstructed every attempt to reform the government; that little member has repeatedly disobeyed and counteracted the general authority, nay, has even supplied the enemies of its country with provisions. Twelve States had agreed to certain improvements which were proposed, being thought absolutely necessary to preserve the existence of the general government; but as these improvements, though really indispensable, could not, by the Confederation, be introduced into it without the consent of every State, the refractory dissent of that little State prevented their adoption. . . . Would the honorable gentleman agree to continue the most radical defects in the old system because the petty State of Rhode Island would not agree to remove them?

He next objects to the exclusive legislation over the district where the seat of the government may be fired. Would he submit that the representatives of this State should carry on their deliberations under the control of any one member of the Union? If any State had the power of legislation over the place where Congress should fix the general government, it would impair the dignity and hazard the safety of Congress. If the safety of the Union were under the control of any particular State, would not foreign corruption probably prevail in such a State, to induce it to exert its controlling influence over the members of the general government? Gentlemen cannot have forgotten the disgraceful insult which Congress received some years ago. And, sir, when we also reflect that the previous cession of particular States is necessary before Congress can legislate exclusively anywhere, we must, instead of being alarmed at this part, heartily approve of it.

But the honorable member sees great danger in the provision concerning the militia. Now, sir, this I conceive to be an additional security to our liberties, without diminishing the power of the States in any considerable degree; it appears to me so highly expedient that I should imagine it would have found advocates even in the warmest friends of the present system. The authority of training the militia and appointing the officers is reserved to the States. But Congress ought to have the power of establishing a uniform system of discipline throughout the States, and to provide for the execution of the laws, suppress insurrections, and repel invasions. These are the only cases wherein they can interfere with the militia; and the obvious necessity of their having power over them in these cases must flash conviction on any reflecting mind. Without uniformity of discipline, military bodies would be incapable of action; without a general controlling power to call forth the strength of the Union, for the purpose of repelling invasions, the country might be overrun and conquered by foreign enemies. Without such a power to suppress insurrections, our liberties might be destroyed by intestine faction, and domestic tyranny be established. . . .

Give me leave to say something of the nature of the government, and to show that it is perfectly safe and just to vest it with the power of taxation. There are a number of opinions; but the principal question is whether it be a federal or a consolidated government. . . . I myself conceive that it is of a mixed nature; it is, in a manner, unprecedented. We cannot find one express prototype in the experience of the world - it stands by itself. In some respects, it is a government of a federal nature; in others, it is of a consolidated nature. Even if we attend to the manner in which the Constitution is investigated, ratified, and made the act of the people of America, I can say, notwithstanding what the honorable gentleman has alleged, that this government is not completely consolidated, nor is it entirely federal. Who are the parties to it? The people - not the people as composing one great body, but the people as composing thirteen sovereignties. Were it, as the gentleman asserts, a consolidated government, the assent of a majority of the people would be sufficient for its establishment, and as a majority have adopted it already, the remaining States would be bound by the act of the majority, even if they unanimously reprobated it. Were it such a government as is suggested, it would be now binding on the people of this State, without having had the privilege of deliberating upon it; but, sir, no State is bound by it, as it is, without its own consent.

Should all the States adopt it, it will be then a government established by the thirteen States of America, not through the intervention of the Legislatures, but by the people at large. In this particular respect, the distinction between the existing and proposed governments is very material. The existing system has been derived from the dependent, derivative authority of the Legislatures of the States, whereas this is derived from the superior power of the people. If we look at the manner in which alterations are to be made in it, the same idea is in some degree attended to. By the new system, a majority of the States cannot introduce amendments; nor are all the States required for that purpose;

three-fourths of them must concur in alterations; in this there is a departure from the federal idea.

The members to the national House of Representatives are to be chosen by the people at large, in proportion to the numbers in the respective districts. When we come to the Senate, its members are elected by the States in their equal and political capacity; but had the government been completely consolidated, the Senate would have been chosen by the people, in their individual capacity, in the same manner as the members of the other House. Thus it is of complicated nature, and this complication, I trust, will be found to exclude the evils of absolute consolidation, as well as of a mere confederacy. If Virginia were separated from all the States, her power and authority would extend to all cases; in like manner, were all powers vested in the general government, it would be a consolidated government; but the powers of the Federal government are enumerated; it can only operate in certain cases; it has legislative powers on defined and limited objects, beyond which it cannot extend its jurisdiction.

But the honorable member has satirized, with peculiar acrimony, the power given to the general government by this Constitution. I conceive that the first question on this subject is whether these powers be necessary; if they be, we are reduced to the dilemma of either submitting to the inconvenience, or losing the Union. Let us consider the most important of these reprobated powers; that of direct taxation is most generally objected to. With respect to the exigencies of government, there is no question but the most easy mode of providing for them will be adopted. When, therefore, direct taxes are not necessary, they will not be recurred to. It can be of little advantage to those in power to raise money in a manner oppressive to the people. To consult the conveniences of the people will cost them nothing, and in many respects will be advantageous to them. Direct taxes will only be recurred to for great purposes. What has brought on other nations those immense debts, under the pressure of which many of them labor? Not the expenses of their governments, but war. If this country should be engaged in war (and I conceive we ought to provide for the possibility of such a case), how would it be carried on? By the usual means provided from year to year? As our imports will be necessary for the expenses of government, and other common exigencies, how are we to carry on the means of defense? How is it possible a war could be supported without money or credit? And would it be possible for government to have credit, without having the power of raising money? No, it would be impossible for any government, in such a case, to defend itself. Then, I say, sir, that it is necessary to establish funds for extraordinary exigencies, and give this power to the general government, for the utter inutility of previous requisitions on the States is too well known.

Would it be possible for those countries, whose finances and revenues are carried to the highest perfection, to carry on the operations of government on great emergencies, such as the maintenance of a war, without an uncontrolled power of raising money? . . . It has been the case in many countries, and no government can exist unless its powers extend to make provisions for every contingency. If we were actually attacked by a powerful nation, and our general government had not the power of raising money, but depended solely on requisitions, our condition would be truly deplorable; if the revenues of this commonwealth were to depend on twenty distinct authorities, it would be impossible for it to carry on its operations. This must be obvious to every member here; I think, therefore, that it is necessary for the preservation of the Union that this power should be given to the general government.

But it is urged that its consolidated nature, joined to the power of direct taxation, will give it a tendency to destroy all subordinate authority, that its increasing influence will speedily enable it to absorb the State governments. I cannot bring myself to think that this will be the case. If the general government were wholly independent of the governments of the particular States, then, indeed, usurpation might be expected to the fullest extent; but, sir, on whom does this general government depend? It derives its authority from these governments, and from the same sources from which their authority is derived. The members of the Federal Government are taken from the same men from whom those of the State Legislatures are taken. If we consider the mode in which the Federal Representatives will be chosen, we shall be convinced that the general never will destroy the individual governments; and this conviction must be strengthened by an attention to the construction of the Senate. The Representatives will be chosen, probably under the influence of the State Legislatures; but there is not the least probability that the election of the latter will be influenced by the former. One hundred and sixty members, representing this commonwealth in one branch of the Legislature, are drawn from the people at large, and must ever possess more influence than the few men who will be elected to the general Legislature. Those who wish to become Federal Representatives must depend on their credit with that class of men who will be the most popular in their counties, who generally represent the people in the State governments; they can, therefore, never succeed in any measure contrary to the wishes of those on whom they depend. So that, on the whole, it is almost certain that the deliberations of the members of the Federal House of

Representatives will be directed to the interests of the people of America.

As to the other branch, the Senators will be appointed by the Legislatures, and, though elected for six years, I do not conceive they will so soon forget the source whence they derive their political existence. This election of one branch of the Federal by the State Legislatures secures an absolute dependence of the former on the latter. The biennial exclusion of one-third will lessen the facility of a combination, and preclude all likelihood of intrigues. . . . Sir, I pledge myself that this government will answer the expectations of its friends, and foil the apprehensions of its enemies. I am persuaded that the patriotism of the people will continue, and be a sufficient guard to their liberties, and that the tendency of the Constitution will be that the State governments will counteract the general interest, and ultimately prevail. The number of the Representatives is yet sufficient for our safety, and will gradually increase; and if we consider their different sources of information, the number will not appear too small.

Sir, that part of the proposed Constitution which gives the general government the power of laying and collecting taxes is indispensable and essential to the existence of any efficient or well-organized system of government; if we consult reason, and be ruled by its dictates, we shall find its justification there, if we review the experience we have had, or contemplate the history of nations, there too we shall find ample reasons to prove its expediency. It would be preposterous to depend for necessary supplies on a body which is fully possessed of the power of withholding them. If a government depends on other governments for its revenues, if it must depend on the voluntary contributions of its members, its existence must be precarious. A government that relies on thirteen independent sovereignties for the means of its existence is a solecism in theory, and a mere nullity in practice. Is it consistent with reason that such a government can promote the happiness of any people? It is subversive of every principle of sound policy to trust the safety of a community with a government totally destitute of the means of protecting itself or its members. Can Congress, after the repeated unequivocal proofs it has experienced of the utter inutility and inefficacy of requisitions, reasonably expect that they would be hereafter effectual or productive? Will not the same local interests, and other causes, militate against a compliance? Whoever hopes the contrary must forever be disappointed. The effect, sir, cannot be changed without a removal of the cause.

Let each county in this commonwealth be supposed free and independent; let your revenues depend on requisitions of proportionate quotas from them; let application be made to them repeatedly, and then ask yourself, is it to be presumed that they would comply, or that an adequate collection could be made from partial compliances? It is now difficult to collect the taxes from them; how much would that difficulty be enhanced, were you to depend solely on their generosity?

I appeal to the reason of every gentleman here, and to his candor, to say whether he is not persuaded that the present confederation is as feeble as the government of Virginia would be in that case; to the same reason I appeal, whether it be compatible with prudence to continue a government of such manifest and palpable weakness and inefficiency.

James Madison

Afterward

The next day, in the handwritten record of the Convention, the reporter noted, *Mr. Madison speaks so low that he cannot be heard.* Ill from exhaustion, Madison was carried to his bed and, under doctor's orders, remained there until June 11, when he once again returned to lead the ratification fight. On June 26, 1788, the Virginia Ratifying Convention voted 89-79 in favor of the Constitution.

Madison served in the House of Representatives where, on September 28, 1789, he proposed twelve Amendments to the U.S. Constitution. The first ten Amendments were ratified in 1791 and are known collectively as the Bill of Rights. President Jefferson appointed James Madison Secretary of State in 1801 and he held that position until his election as President of the United States in 1809. Madison served two terms as President. The major event of his eight-year Presidency was the War of 1812. In 1817 Madison retired to Montpelier, where he died, at the age of eighty-five, on June 28, 1836.

Selected Reading

Banning, Lance, *The Sacred Fire of Liberty: James Madison and the Founding of the Republic*, 1995.

Brant, Irving, *The Fourth President: A Life of James Madison*, 1970.

Hunt, Gaillard, *The Life of James Madison*, 1968.

Peterson, Merrill D., Editor, *James Madison: A Biography in His Own Words*, 1974.

Rutland, Robert, *James Madison: The Founding Father*, 1987.

Schultz, Harold S., *James Madison*, 1970.

Increase Mather
An Arrow Against Mixed Dancing
February 16, 1685

To everything there is a season, and a time to every purpose under heaven - a time to be born, and a time to die - a time to plant, and a time to pluck up that which is planted - a time to kill, and a time to heal - a time to break down, and a time to build up - a time to weep, and a time to laugh - a time to mourn, and a time to dance.

- Ecclesiastes 3:1-4

Dancers are wont to allege that Scripture, Ecclesiastes 3:4 - "There is a time to dance"- [makes their mixed dancing lawful]. That does not speak a syllable for the justification of such dancing nor any other dancing, since the meaning of the [passage] is not that it is a lawful time, but only a limited time. **- Increase Mather (1685)**

Increase Mather was born at Dorchester, Massachusetts, on June 21, 1639, the son of the Reverend Richard and Katherine (Holt) Mather. Educated at Harvard College in Cambridge, Massachusetts and Trinity College in Dublin, Ireland, the Reverend Mather took the pulpit of Boston's Old North Church in 1681.

Contemporary accounts of Increase Mather's sermons said he was, *A most excellent preacher, using great plainness of speech, with much light, and heat and force and power. . . . His delivery had something singular in it. He spoke with a grave and wise deliberation; but on some subjects, his voice would rise for the more emphatical clauses, as the discourse went on, and anon come on with such tonitruous cogency, that the hearers would be struck with awe, like what would be produced on the fall of thunderbolts.*

To Boston's great Puritan minister, the Reverend Increase Mather, *mixed or promiscuous dancing* was impure - an act of adultery. On February 16, 1685, Reverend Mather gave this landmark sermon, *An Arrow Against Profane and Promiscuous Dancing Drawn out of the Quiver of the Scriptures.*

Concerning the controversy about dancing, the question is not whether all dancing be in itself sinful. . . . Nor is the question whether a sober and grave dancing of men with men, or of women with women, be not allowable; we make no doubt of that, where it may be done without offense, in due season, and with moderation. The Prince of Philosophers has observed truly that dancing . . . is a natural expression of joy, so that there is no more sin in it than in laughter or any outward expression of inward rejoicing.

But our question is concerning . . . that which is commonly called mixed or promiscuous dancing, [that is,] of men and women (be they elder or younger persons) together. Now this we affirm to be utterly unlawful and that it cannot be tolerated in such a place as New England without great sin. And that it may appear that we are not transported by affection without judgment, let the following arguments be weighed in the balance of the sanctuary.

That which the Scripture condemns is sinful. None but atheists will deny this proposition. . . . [T]he Scripture condemns promiscuous dancing. This assumption is proved from the Seventh Commandment [Thou shall not commit adultery]. It is an eternal truth to be observed in expounding the commandment that whenever any sin is forbidden, not only the highest acts of that sin, but all degrees thereof, and all occasions leading thereto, are prohibited. . . . [P]romiscuous dancing, as a breach of the Seventh Commandment, . . . is evil in the sight of God. . . .

How often does the Scripture commend unto Christians gravity and sobriety in their behavior at all times, and condemn all levity in carriage. . . . [D]ancing is (as some have expressed it) a regular madness. [A wise Bishop], after he had seen such things, the question being asked, *What is the difference between a dancer and a madman?* replied, *There was no other difference, but only this, that the person who is really frantic is mad all the day long, [whereas] the dancer is only mad an hour in a day.* . . . And truly such affected levity and antic behavior, when persons skip and fling about like bedlams, as they say dancers are wont to do, is no way becoming the gravity of a Christian. . . .

If we consider by whom this practice of promiscuous dancing was first invented, by whom patronized, and by whom witnessed against, we may well conclude that the admitting of it in such a place as New England will be a thing pleasing to the Devil, but highly provoking to the Holy God. Who were the inventors of petulant dancing? They had not their original amongst the people of God, but amongst the heathen. Learned men have well observed that the Devil was the first inventor of the impleaded dances, and the [heathens] who worshipped him the first practitioners in this art. . . . A practice in use only amongst the heathen, but never known among the people of God, except in times of degeneracy, ought not to be taken up. But this is true of that practice which we now testify against.

By whom have promiscuous dances been patronized? Truly, by the worst of the heathen and such like atheists . . . delighted in them. . . . [A] learned man . . . was indeed clearly convinced of the great sin which is therein. His words are worthy our taking notice of them; he thus expresseth himself, *The entering into the processions of dances hinders men from ingress into the heavenly procession; and those who dance offend against the sacraments of the Church. First, against baptism - they break the covenant which they made with God in baptism, wherein they promised to renounce the Devil and his pomps; but when they enter into the dance, they go in the pompous procession of the Devil.*

. . . . [The] Saints of God, and Martyrs of Jesus, were haters of mixed dances. . . . They thus testify, *A dance is the devil's procession. He that enters into a dance enters into his possession. The Devil is the guide, the middle and the end of the dance. A man sinneth in dancing diverse ways, as in his pace, for all his steps are numbered - in his touch, in his ornaments, in his hearing, sight, speech, and other vanities.* . . . *[H]ow wicked a thing it is to dance. He that danceth maintaineth the Devil's pomp and singeth his Mass. Again, in a dance, a man breaks the Ten Commandments of God. The very motion of the body which is used in dancing giveth testimony enough of evil. [It is said] the miserable dancer knoweth not that as many paces as he makes in dancing, so many steps he makes to Hell.* Thus (and much more to this purpose) do those faithful witnesses of Christ declare against this profane practice. . . .

[S]hall Christians, who have the Scriptures and the glorious light of the Gospel to illuminate them, practice or plead for such works of darkness? And shall that abomination be set up in New England (the place where the light of the Gospel has shined so gloriously) which moral heathen have detested? The Lord lay not this great sin to the charge of any who have at all been guilty of it.

. . . . A Christian should do nothing wherein he cannot exercise grace or put a respect of obedience to God on what he does. This in lawful recreations may be done. But who can seriously pray to the Holy God to be with him when he is going to a promiscuous dance? It is that which hinders religious exercises, especially for persons to go immediately from hearing a sermon to a [mixed] dance. It is a high degree of profaneness and impudent contempt put upon the Gospel. The Devil thereby catcheth away the good seed of the Word, and the former religious exercise is rendered ineffectual. Some that write against dances observe that many young persons who seemed to be hopeful, and to have some good beginnings of piety in them, by falling into acquaintance with that unlawful recreation, have in a little time utterly left all favor of good, it being just with God, when they have forsaken him to follow the Devil's pomps and vanities, to withdraw his Holy Spirit from them, and judicially give them up to mind nothing else but folly. The Lord grant that none amongst ourselves may find the observation true.

. . . . It is known from their own confessions that amongst the Indians in this America, oftentimes at their dances the Devil appears in bodily shape and takes away one of them alive. In some places of this wilderness there are great heaps of stones, which the Indians have laid together as a horrid remembrance of so hideous a fruit of their satanical dances. . . .

Not that dancing or music or singing are in themselves sinful, but if the dancing master be wicked they are commonly abused to lasciviousness, and that makes them to become abominable. But will you that are professors of religion have your children to be thus taught? The Lord expects that you should give the children who are baptized into His name another kind of education, that you should bring them up in the nurture and admonition of the Lord. And do you not hear the Lord expostulating the case with you and saying, you have taken my children, the children that were given unto me, the children that were solemnly engaged to renounce the pomps of Satan; but is this a light matter that you have taken these my children, and initiated them in the pomps and vanities of the Wicked One, contrary to your covenant? What will you say in the day of the Lord's pleading with you? We have that charity for you as to believe that you have erred through ignorance and not wickedly; and we have therefore accounted it our duty to inform you in the truth. If you resolve not on reformation, you will be left inexcusable. However it shall be, we have now given our testimony and delivered our own souls. Consider what we say, and the Lord will give you understanding in all things.

Afterward

Mixed dancing soon became the least of Increase Mather's problems. In 1686 King Charles II revoked the Royal Charters of all the New England Colonies (Maine, New Hampshire, Massachusetts, Rhode Island, Connecticut, New York, and New Jersey), creating in their place the Dominion of New England. For over fifty-five years, the Massachusetts Bay Colony had been governed exclusively by and for Puritans. The Puritans rebelled at the loss of their political independence. Increase Mather led the rebellion. On December 24, 1686, the Royal Governor of the Dominion of New England, in charge of the civil and religious life of the Colonies, arrested and imprisoned the Reverend Mather on a charge of *sedition & treason*. On January 31, 1687, a Boston jury freed him. Upon his release, Mather told his Old North Church Congregation, *When God is for a man, they that are against him shall do no good.*

Increase Mather died on August 23, 1723 at age eighty-four, having served as Minister of Boston's Old North Church for forty-two years.

Selected Reading

Hall, Michael G., Editor, *The Autobiography of Increase Mather*, 1962.

———, *The Last American Puritan: The Life of Increase Mather*, 1988.

Lowance, Mason I., Jr., *Increase Mather*, 1974.

Mather, Cotton, *Memoirs of the Life of the Late Reverend Increase Mather*, 1725.

Murdock, Kenneth, *Increase Mather*, 1925.

James Otis
A Man's House Is His Castle
February 24, 1761

GEORGE II, by the Grace of God, KING

Know ye it is declared that our customs officials are authorized [under this Writ of Assistance] to go aboard any ship, inbound or outbound, or enter any house or warehouse, and in the case of resistance to break open doors, to search for and seize any goods or merchandise whatsoever prohibited and uncustomed. **- The Writ of Assistance**

In 1755 the Superior Court of Massachusetts issued a *Writ of Assistance*, a general search warrant authorizing English customs officials to arbitrarily search for and seize any goods that they believed merchants had illegally imported into Massachusetts. Under English law, the Writ of Assistance was to stay in force until the death of George II, when it had to be reissued in the name of the new King within six months to stay in force.

In 1760 *The Sarah* was boarded, seized, and sold by customs officials for carrying an uncustomed (untaxed) cargo. The owner hired Boston lawyer James Otis to defend him against this application of the Writ of Assistance.

James Otis, Jr. was born on February 5, 1724 in Barnstable, Massachusetts, the son of James and Mary (Allyne) Otis. Educated at Harvard College, Otis graduated in 1743. He then studied the law and was admitted to the Massachusetts bar in 1748.

On behalf of *The Sarah's* owners, James Otis sued Boston's customs officials for recovery of their lost property. The legality of the Writ of Assistance was upheld and Otis lost the case. When England's King George II died, Otis seized the opportunity and, representing the Boston Merchants Society, moved to block the writ's renewal, thus allowing it to expire. On February 24, 1761, James Otis closed his case with this landmark speech.

May it please your Honors, I was desired by one of the court to look into the books, and consider the question now before them concerning writs of assistance. I have, accordingly, considered it, and now appear not only in obedience to your order, but likewise in behalf of the inhabitants of this town, who have presented another petition, and out of regard to the liberties of the subject. And I take this opportunity to declare that, whether under a fee or not (for in such a cause as this I despise a fee), I will to my dying day oppose with all the powers and faculties God has given me all such instruments of slavery, on the one hand, and villainy, on the other, as this writ of assistance is.

It appears to me the worst instrument of arbitrary power, the most destructive of English liberty and the fundamental principles of law, that ever was found in an English law book. I must, therefore, beg your Honors' patience and attention to the whole range of an argument that may, perhaps, appear uncommon in many things, as well as to points of learning that are more remote and unusual - that the whole tendency of my design may the more easily be perceived, the conclusions better descend, and the force of them be better felt. I shall not think much of my pains in this cause, as I engaged in it from principle. I was solicited to argue this cause as Advocate General; and because I would not I have been charged with desertion from my office. To this charge I can give a very sufficient answer. I renounced that office, and I argue this cause from the same principle; and I argue it with the greater pleasure, as it is in favor of British liberty at a time when we hear the greatest monarch upon earth declaring from his throne that he glories in the name of Briton, and that the privileges of his people are dearer to him than the most valuable prerogatives of his crown; and it is in opposition to a kind of power, the exercise of which, in former periods of English history, cost one king of England his head and another his throne. I have taken more pains in this cause than I ever will take again, although my engaging in this and another popular cause has raised much resentment. But I think I can sincerely declare that I cheerfully submit myself to every odious name for conscience sake; and from my soul I despise all those whose guilt, malice, or folly has made them my foes. Let the consequences be what they will, I am determined to proceed. The only principles of public conduct that are worthy of a gentleman or a man are to sacrifice estate, ease, health, and applause, and even life, to the sacred calls of his country.

These manly sentiments, in private life, make the good citizen - in public life, the patriot and the hero. I do not say that when brought to the test I shall be invincible. I pray God I may never be brought to the melancholy trial; but if ever I should, it will be then known how far I can reduce to practice principles which I know to be founded in truth. In the meantime I will proceed to the subject of this writ.

Your Honors will find in the old books concerning the office of a Justice of the Peace precedents of general warrants to search suspected houses. But in more modern books you will find only special warrants to search such and such houses, specially named, in which the complainant has before sworn that he suspects his goods are concealed, and will find it adjudged that special warrants only are legal. In the same manner I rely on it that the writ prayed for in this petition, being general, is illegal. It is a power that places the liberty of every man in the hands of every petty officer. I say I admit that special writs of assistance, to search special places, may be granted to certain persons on oath; but I deny that the writ now prayed for can be granted, for I beg leave to make some observations on the writ itself before I proceed to other acts of Parliament. In the first place, the writ is universal, being directed *to all and singular justices, sheriffs, constables, and all other officers and subjects*, so that, in short, it is directed to every subject in the King's dominions. Everyone with this writ may be a tyrant in a legal manner, also may control, imprison, or murder anyone within the realm. In the next place, it is perpetual; there is no return. A man is accountable to no person for his doings. Every man may reign secure in his petty tyranny and spread terror and desolation around him, until the trump of the archangel shall excite different emotions in his soul. In the third place, a person with this writ, in the daytime, may enter all houses, shops, etc., at will, and command all to assist him. Fourthly, by this writ, not only deputies, etc., but even their menial servants are allowed to lord it over us. What is this but to have the curse of Canaan with a witness on us - to be the servant of servants, the most despicable of God's creation?

Now, one of the most essential branches of English liberty is the freedom of one's house. A man's house is his castle; and whilst he is quiet, he is as well guarded as a prince in his castle. This writ, if it should be declared legal, would totally annihilate this privilege. Custom house officers may enter our houses when they please; we are commanded to permit their entry. Their menial servants may enter, may break locks, bars, and everything in their way; and whether they break through malice or revenge, no man, no court, can inquire. Bare suspicion without oath is sufficient. This wanton exercise of this power is not a chimerical suggestion of a heated brain.

I will mention some facts. Mr. Pew had one of these writs, and when Mr. Ware succeeded him, he endorsed this writ over to Mr. Ware, so that these writs are negotiable from one officer to another, and so your Honors have no opportunity of judging the persons to whom this vast power is delegated. Another instance is this - Mr. Justice Walley had called this same Mr. Ware before him, by a constable, to answer for a breach of the Sabbath Day acts or that of profane swearing. As soon as he had finished, Mr. Ware asked him if he had done. He replied, *Yes*. *Well, then*, said Mr. Ware, *I will show you a little of my power. I command you to permit me to search your house for uncustomed goods*, and went on to search the house from the garret to the cellar, and then served the constable in the same manner! But to show another absurdity in this writ, if it should be established, I insist upon it every person, by the 14th of Charles II, has this power as well as the custom house officers. The words are, *It shall be lawful for any person or persons authorized*, etc. What a scene does this open! Every man, prompted by revenge, ill humor, or wantonness to inspect the inside of his neighbor's house may get a writ of assistance. Others will ask it from self-defense; one arbitrary exertion will provoke another, until society be involved in tumult and in blood.

[No further text of James Otis' A Man's House Is His Castle speech exists. John Adams, present in court that day, later wrote that after this opening statement Otis made four separate arguments which Adams reported as follows:]

One. Otis asserted that every man, merely natural, was an independent sovereign, subject to no law but the law written on his heart and revealed to him by his Maker, in the constitution of his nature, and the inspiration of his understanding and his conscience. His right to his life, his liberty, no created being could rightfully contest. Nor was his right to his property less incontestable. The club that he had snapped from a tree, for a staff or for defense, was his own. His bow and arrow were his own; if by a pebble he had killed a partridge or a squirrel, it was his own. No creature, man or beast, had a right to take it from him. If he had taken an eel, or a smelt, or a sculpin, it was his property. In short, he sported upon this topic with so much wit and humor, and at the same time with so much indisputable truth and reason, that he was not less entertaining than instructive. Otis asserted that these rights were inherent and inalienable, that they never could be surrendered or alienated, but by idiots or madmen, and all the acts of idiots and lunatics were void, and not obligatory, by all the laws of God and man. Nor were the poor Negroes forgotten. Not a Quaker in Philadelphia, or Mr. Jefferson in Virginia, ever asserted the rights of Negroes in stronger terms. Young as I was, and ignorant as I was, I shuddered at the doctrine he taught; and I have all my life shuddered, and still shudder, at the consequences that may be drawn from such premises. Shall we say that the rights of masters and servants clash and can be decided only by force? I adore the idea of gradual abolitions! but who shall decide how fast or how slowly these abolitions shall be made?

Two. From individual independence Otis proceeded to association. If it was inconsistent with the dignity of human nature to say that men were gregarious animals, like wild geese, it surely could offend no delicacy to say they were social animals by nature - that there were natural sympathies, and, above all, the sweet attraction of the sexes, which must soon draw them together in little groups, and by degrees in larger congregations, for mutual assistance and defense. And this must have happened before any formal covenant, by express words or signs, was concluded. When general councils and deliberations commenced, the objects could be no other than the mutual defense and security of every individual for his life, his liberty, and his property. To suppose them to have surrendered these in any other way than by equal rules and general consent was to suppose them idiots or madmen, whose acts were never binding. To suppose them surprised by fraud, or compelled by force into any other compact, such fraud and such force could confer no obligation. Every man had a right to trample it under foot whenever he pleased. In short, he asserted these rights to be derived only from nature and the Author of Nature - that they were inherent, inalienable, and indefeasible by any laws, pacts, contracts, covenants, or stipulations which man could devise.

Three. These principles and these rights were wrought into the English Constitution as fundamental laws. And under this head Otis went back to the old Saxon laws, and to Magna Carta, and the fifty confirmations of it in Parliament, and the executions ordained against the violators of it, and the national vengeance which had been taken on them from time to time, down to the Jameses and Charleses, and to the position of rights and the Bill of Rights and the Revolution. Otis asserted that the security of these rights to life, liberty, and property had been the object of all those struggles against arbitrary power - temporal and spiritual, civil and political, military and ecclesiastical - in every age. Otis asserted that our ancestors, as British subjects, and we, their descendants, as British subjects, were entitled to all those rights by the British Constitution, as well as by the law of nature and our provincial character, as much as any inhabitant of London or Bristol, or any part of England, and were not to be cheated out of them by any phantom of *virtual representation*, or any other fiction of law or politics, or any monkish trick of deceit and hypocrisy.

Four. Otis then examined the acts of trade, one by one, and demonstrated that if they were considered as revenue laws, they destroyed all our security of property, liberty, and life, every right of nature, and the English Constitution, and the charter of the province. Here Otis considered the distinction between *external and internal taxes*, at that time a popular and commonplace distinction. But Otis asserted that there was no such distinction in theory or upon any principle but *necessity*. The necessity that the commerce of the empire should be under one direction was obvious. The Americans had been so sensible of this necessity that they had connived at the distinction between external and internal taxes and had submitted to the acts of trade as regulations of commerce, but never as taxations or revenue laws. Nor had the British Government till now ever dared to attempt to enforce them as taxations or revenue laws. They had lain dormant in that character for a century almost. The Navigation Act he allowed to be binding upon us, because we had consented to it by our own legislature. Here Otis gave a history of the Navigation Act of the 1st of Charles II, a plagiarism from Oliver Cromwell. This act had lain dormant for fifteen years. In 1675, after repeated letters and orders from the king, Governor Leverett very candidly informs his Majesty that the law had not been executed because it was thought unconstitutional, Parliament not having authority over us.

Afterward

John Adams, then just twenty-four, was sitting in the courtroom on February 24, 1761, when James Otis delivered this speech. In 1817 Adams recalled in a letter, *Otis was a flame of fire! American independence was then and there born; the seed of patriots and heroes was then and there sown. Every man of the crowded audience appeared to me to go away, as I did, ready to take up arms against the writs of assistance. Then and there was the first scene of the first act of opposition to the arbitrary claims of Great Britain.*

There and then the child of Independence was born. In fifteen years, namely 1776, he grew up to manhood and declared himself free.

The Chief Justice of Massachusetts, unwilling to rule either against the King's customs officials or the popular sentiment of the people of Boston, recessed the case and sent to England for further instructions. In 1766 the Attorney General of England ruled that Parliament had never specifically authorized the issuance of writs of assistance in the American colonies.

James Otis, described by his friends as *fiery and passionate* and his enemies as *rash and turbulent*, is credited with coining the phrase, *Taxation without representation is tyranny!* After the trial, he wrote political pamphlets, including 1762's *Vindication of Massachusetts Bay*, 1764's *The Rights of the British Colonies Asserted and Proved*, 1765's *Vindication of the British Colonies*, and (with Samuel Adams) 1768's *Massachusetts Circular Letter*. He spoke out on political subjects - *Every British subject in America is of common right, by Acts of Parliament, and by the laws of God and nature, entitled to all the essential privileges of Britons*. He served the cause of American independence, alongside his friends and fellow Sons of Liberty, John and Samuel Adams, until the night of September 5, 1769, when he was brutally beaten by his political enemies and left incapacitated. John Adams later referred to the beating as *the assassination* of James Otis.

James Otis died on May 23, 1783.

Selected Reading

Galvin, John, *Three Men of Boston*, 1976.
Ridpath, John C., *James Otis, the Pre-Revolutionist*, 1898.
Tudor, William, *The Life of James Otis of Massachusetts*, 1970.

Thomas Paine
These Are The Times That Try Men's Souls
December 25, 1776

Without the pen of Thomas Paine the sword of George Washington would have been raised in vain.   - **John Adams**

On January 10, 1776, an anonymous political pamphlet, *Common Sense*, appeared for sale in the bookstores of Philadelphia. It argued passionately for the complete independence of the American Colonies from Great Britain. In the next three months, *Common Sense* sold an estimated 120,000 copies. The author of *Common Sense* was the then little known Thomas Paine.

Thomas Paine was born on January 29, 1737 in Thetford, England, the son of Joseph and Frances (Cocke) Paine. He was a self-educated, radical writer and activist who lived and worked in obscurity in London. Paine met Benjamin Franklin, who urged him to go to America. Franklin, in a letter of introduction, called Paine *an ingenious and worthy young man.*

Paine arrived in Philadelphia on November 30, 1774 and began writing political commentary for *The Pennsylvania Magazine* and *The Pennsylvania Journal.* In late 1775 Paine began writing a radical political pamphlet entitled *Plain Truth* (later re-entitled *Common Sense*). Paine joined the Continental Army and, upon witnessing the capture of New York City's Fort Washington by the British and the long retreat of the Army to Philadelphia, he wrote words to inspire the Army in battle. The result was the first installment of *The American Crisis.* Published in *The Pennsylvania Journal* on December 19, 1776, Paine's landmark words electrified all those who read them, including George Washington, who, on Christmas Day, 1776, ordered his officers to read them to the entire Army.

These are the times that try men's souls. The summer soldier and the sunshine patriot will, in this crisis, shrink from the service of their country; but he that stands it now deserves the love and thanks of man and woman. Tyranny, like hell, is not easily conquered - yet we have this consolation with us, that the harder the conflict, the more glorious the triumph. What we obtain too cheap, we esteem too lightly; it is darkness only that gives everything its value. Heaven knows how to put a proper price upon its goods, and it would be strange indeed if so celestial an article as freedom should not be highly rated. Britain, with an army to enforce her tyranny, has declared that she has a right not only to tax but *bind us in all cases whatsoever*, and if being bound in that manner is not slavery, then there is not such a thing as slavery upon earth. Even the expression is impious, for so unlimited a power can belong only to God.

Whether the independence of the continent was declared too soon or delayed too long, I will not now enter into an argument; my own simple opinion is that had it been eight months earlier, it would have been much better. We did not make a proper use of last winter (neither could we) while we were in a dependent state. However, the fault, if it were one, was all our own; we have none to blame but ourselves. But no great deal is lost yet. All that Howe has been doing for this month past is rather a ravage than a conquest, which the spirit of the Jerseys a year ago would have quickly repulsed, and which time and a little resolution will soon recover.

I have as little superstition in me as any man living, but my secret opinion has ever been, and still is, that God Almighty will not give up a people to military destruction, or leave them unsupportedly to perish, who have so earnestly and so repeatedly sought to avoid the calamities of war by every decent method which wisdom could invent. Neither have I so much of the infidel in me as to suppose that He has relinquished the government of the world and given us up to the care of devils; and, as I do not, I cannot see on what grounds the king of Britain can look up to heaven for help against us - a common murderer, a highwayman, or a house-breaker has as good a pretense as he.

'Tis surprising to see how rapidly a panic will sometimes run through a country. All nations and ages have been subject to them. Britain has trembled like an ague at the report of a French fleet of flat-bottomed boats; and in the fourteenth century the whole English army, after ravaging the kingdom of France, was driven back like men petrified with fear - and this brave exploit was performed by a few broken forces collected and headed by a woman, Joan of Arc. Would that heaven might inspire some Jersey maid to espirit up her countrymen and save her fair fellow sufferers from ravage and ravishment! Yet panics (in some cases) have their uses; they produce as much good as hurt. Their duration is always short; the mind soon grows through them and acquires a firmer habit than before. But their peculiar advantage is that they are the touchstones of sincerity and hypocrisy and bring things and men to light which might otherwise have lain forever undiscovered. In fact, they have the same effect on secret traitors which an imaginary apparition would have upon a private murderer. They sift out the hidden thoughts of man, and hold them up in public to the world. Many a disguised Tory has lately shown his head, that shall penitentially solemnize with curses the day on which Howe arrived upon the Delaware.

As I was with the troops at Fort Lee and marched with them to the edge of Pennsylvania, I am well acquainted with many circumstances which those who live at a distance know but little or nothing of. Our situation there was exceedingly cramped, the place being a narrow neck of land between the North River and the Hackensack. Our force was inconsiderable, being not one-fourth so great as Howe could bring against us. We had no army at hand to have relieved the garrison, had we shut ourselves up and stood on our defense. Our ammunition, light artillery, and the best part of our stores had been removed, on the apprehension that Howe would endeavor to penetrate the Jerseys, in which case Fort Lee could be of no use to us, for it must occur to every thinking man, whether in the army or not, that these kinds of field forts are only for temporary purposes and last in use no longer than the enemy directs his force against the particular object which such forts are raised to defend. Such was our situation and condition at Fort Lee on the morning of the 20th of November, when an officer arrived with information that the enemy with 200 boats had landed about seven miles above; Major General [Nathaniel] Greene, who commanded the garrison, immediately ordered them under arms, and sent express to General Washington at the town of Hackensack, distant by the way of the ferry six miles.

Our first object was to secure the bridge over the Hackensack, which laid up the river between the enemy and us - about six miles from us and three from them. General Washington arrived in about three-quarters of an hour and marched at the head of the troops towards the bridge, which place I expected we should have a brush for; however, they did not choose to dispute it with us, and the greatest part of our troops went over the bridge, the rest over the ferry, except some which passed at a mill on a small creek, between the bridge and the ferry, and made their way through some marshy grounds up to the town of Hackensack, and there passed the river. We brought off as much baggage as the wagons could contain; the rest was lost. The simple object was to bring off the garrison, and march them on till they could be strengthened by the Jersey or Pennsylvania militia so as to be enabled to make a stand.

We stayed four days at Newark, collected our out-posts with some of the Jersey militia, and marched out twice to meet the enemy, on being informed that they were advancing, though our numbers were greatly inferior to theirs. Howe, in my little opinion, committed a great error in generalship in not throwing a body of forces off from Staten Island through Amboy, by which means he might have seized all our stores at Brunswick, and intercepted our march into Pennsylvania; but if we believe the power of hell to be limited, we must likewise believe that their agents are under some providential control.

I shall not now attempt to give all the particulars of our retreat to the Delaware; suffice it for the present to say that both officers and men, though greatly harassed and fatigued, frequently without rest, covering, or provision - the inevitable consequences of a long retreat - bore it with a manly and martial spirit. All their wishes centered in one, which was that the country would turn out and help them to drive the enemy back. Voltaire has remarked that King William never appeared to full advantage but in difficulties and in action; the same remark may be made on General Washington, for the character fits him. There is a natural firmness in some minds which cannot be unlocked by trifles, but which, when unlocked, discovers a cabinet of fortitude; and I reckon it among those kind of public blessings (which we do not immediately see) that God hath blessed him with uninterrupted health and given him a mind that can even flourish upon care.

I shall conclude . . . with some miscellaneous remarks on the state of our affairs, and shall begin with asking the following question - Why is it that the enemy have left the New England provinces, and made these middle ones the seat of war? The answer is easy - New England is not infested with Tories and we are. I have been tender in raising the cry against these men and used numberless arguments to show them their danger, but it will not do to sacrifice a world either to their folly or their baseness. The period is now arrived in which either they or we must change our sentiments or one or both must fall. And what is a Tory? Good God! what is he? I should not be afraid to go with a hundred Whigs against a thousand Tories, were they to attempt to get into arms. Every Tory is a coward, for servile, slavish, self-interested fear is the foundation of Toryism, and a man under such influence, though he may be cruel, never can be brave.

But, before the line of irrecoverable separation be drawn between us, let us reason the matter together. Your conduct is an invitation to the enemy, yet not one in a thousand of you has heart enough to join him. Howe is as much deceived by you as the American cause is injured by you. He expects you will all take up arms, and flock to his standard with muskets on your shoulders. Your opinions are of no use to him unless you support him personally, for 'tis soldiers, and not Tories, that he wants.

I once felt all that kind of anger which a man ought to feel against the mean principles that are held by the Tories. A noted one, who keeps a tavern at Amboy, was standing at his door, with as pretty a child in his hand, about eight or nine years old, as I ever saw, and after speaking his mind as freely as he thought was prudent, finished with this unfatherly expression, *Well! give me peace in my day*. Not a man lives on the continent but fully believes that a separation must some time or other finally take place, and a generous parent should have said, *If there must be trouble, let it be in my day, that my child may have peace,* and this single reflection, well applied, is sufficient to awaken every man to duty. Not a place upon earth might be so happy as America. Her situation is remote from all the wrangling world, and she has nothing to do but to trade with them. A man can distinguish in himself between temper and principle, and I am as confident as I am that God governs the world that America will never be happy till she gets clear of foreign dominion. Wars, without ceasing, will break out till that period arrives, and the continent must in the end be conqueror, for though the flame of liberty may sometimes cease to shine, the coal can never expire.

America did not nor does not want force, but she wanted a proper application of that force. Wisdom is not the purchase of a day, and it is no wonder that we should err at the first setting off. From an excess of tenderness, we were unwilling to raise an army, and trusted our cause to the temporary defense of a well-meaning militia. A summer's experience has now taught us better; yet with those troops, while they were collected, we were able to set bounds to the progress of the enemy, and, thank God! they are again assembling. I always considered militia as the best troops in the world for a sudden exertion, but they will not do for a long campaign. Howe, it is probable, will make an attempt on this city; should he fail on this side the Delaware, he is ruined. If he succeeds, our cause is not ruined. He stakes all on his side against a part on ours; [if] he succeeds, the consequence will be that armies from both ends of the continent will march to assist their suffering friends in the middle states, for he cannot go everywhere - it is impossible. I consider Howe as the greatest enemy the Tories have; he is bringing a war into their country, which, had it not been for him and partly for themselves, they had been clear of. Should he now be expelled, I wish with all the devotion of a Christian that the names of Whig and Tory may never more be mentioned; but should the Tories give him encouragement to come, or assistance if he come, I as sincerely wish that our next year's arms may expel them from the continent, and the Congress appropriate their possessions to the relief of those who have suffered in well-doing. A single successful battle next year will settle the whole. America could carry on a two years' war by the confiscation of the property of disaffected persons, and be made happy by their expulsion. Say not that this is revenge; call it rather the soft resentment of a suffering people, who, having no object in view but the good of all, have staked their own all upon a seemingly doubtful event. Yet it is folly to argue against determined hardness; eloquence may strike the ear, and the language of sorrow draw forth the tear of compassion, but nothing can reach the heart that is steeled with prejudice.

Quitting this class of men, I turn with the warm ardor of a friend to those who have nobly stood, and are yet determined to stand the matter out; I call not upon a few, but upon all, not on this state or that state, but on every state - up and help us - lay your shoulders to the wheel, better have too much force than too little, when so great an object is at stake. Let it be told to the future world that in the depth of winter, when nothing but hope and virtue could survive, that the city and the country, alarmed at one common danger, came forth to meet and to repulse it. Say not that thousands are gone; turn out your tens of thousands; throw not the burden of the day upon Providence, but *show your faith by your works* that God may bless you. It matters not where you live, or what rank of life you hold, the evil or the blessing will reach you all. The far and the near, the home counties and the back, the rich and the poor, will suffer or rejoice alike. The heart that feels not now is dead; the blood of his children will curse his cowardice who shrinks back at a time when a little might have saved the world and made them happy. I love the man that can smile in trouble, that can gather strength from distress, and grow brave by reflection. 'Tis the business of little minds to shrink; but he whose heart is firm, and whose conscience approves his conduct, will pursue his principles unto death. My own line of reasoning is to myself as straight and clear as a ray of light. Not all the treasures of the world, so far as I believe, could have induced me to support an offensive war, for I think it murder; but if a thief breaks into my house, burns and destroys my property, and kills or threatens to kill me or those that are in it, and to *bind me in all cases whatsoever* to his absolute will, am I to suffer it? What signifies it to me whether he who does it is a king or a common man, my countryman or not my countryman, whether it be done by an individual villain or an army of them? If we reason to the root of things we shall find no difference; neither can any just cause be assigned why we should punish in the one case and pardon in the other. Let them call me rebel and welcome, I feel no concern from it; but I should suffer the misery of devils were I to make a whore of my soul by swearing allegiance to one whose character is that of a sottish, stupid, stubborn, worthless, brutish man. I conceive likewise a horrid idea in receiving mercy from a being who at the last day shall be shrieking to the rocks and mountains to cover him, and fleeing with terror from the orphan, the widow, and the slain of America.

There are cases which cannot be overdone by language, and this is one. There are persons, too, who see not the full extent of the evil which threatens them; they solace themselves with hopes that the enemy, if he succeed, will be merciful. It is the madness of folly to expect mercy from those who have refused to do justice; and even mercy, where conquest is the object, is only a trick of war; the cunning of the fox is as murderous as the violence of the wolf, and we ought to guard equally against both. Howe's first object is, partly by threats and partly by promises, to terrify or seduce the people to deliver up their arms and receive mercy. The ministry recommended the same plan to Gage, and this is what the Tories call making their peace, *a peace which passeth all understanding* indeed! A peace which would be the immediate forerunner of a worse ruin than any we have yet thought of. Ye men of Pennsylvania, do reason upon these things! Were the back counties to give up their arms, they would fall an easy prey to the Indians, who are all armed; this perhaps is what some Tories would not be sorry for. Were the home counties to deliver up their arms, they would be exposed to the resentment of the back counties, who would then have it in their power to chastise their defection as pleasure. And were any one state to give up its arms, that the state must be garrisoned by all Howe's army of Britons and Hessians to preserve it from the anger of the rest. Mutual fear is the principal link in the chain of mutual love, and woe be to that state that breaks the compact. Howe is mercifully inviting you to barbarous destruction, and men must be either rogues or fools that will not see it. I dwell upon the vapors of imagination; I bring reason to your ears, and, in language as plain as A, B, C, hold up truth to your eyes.

I thank God that I fear not. I see no real cause for fear. I know our situation well and can see the way out of it. While our army was collected, Howe dared not risk a battle; and it is no credit to him that he decamped from the White Plains and waited a mean opportunity to ravage the defenseless

Jerseys; but it is great credit to us that, with a handful of men, we sustained an orderly retreat for near an hundred miles, brought off our ammunition, all our field pieces, the greatest part of our stores, and had four rivers to pass. None can say that our retreat was precipitate, for we were near three weeks in performing it, that the country might have time to come in. Twice we marched back to meet the enemy and remained out till dark. The sign of fear was not seen in our camp and, had not some of the cowardly and disaffected inhabitants spread false alarms through the country, the Jerseys had never been ravaged. Once more we are again collected and collecting; our new army at both ends of the continent is recruiting fast, and we shall be able to open the next campaign with sixty thousand men, well armed and clothed. This is our situation and who will may know it. By perseverance and fortitude we have the prospect of a glorious issue, by cowardice and submission, the sad choice of a variety of evils - a ravaged country, a depopulated city, habitations without safety, and slavery without hope, our homes turned into barracks and bawdyhouses for Hessians, and a future race to provide for, whose fathers we shall doubt of. Look on this picture and weep over it! and if there yet remains one thoughtless wretch who believes it not, let him suffer it unlamented.

Afterward

By the end of the American Revolution, Thomas Paine had written nine additional parts to *The American Crisis*. In 1787 he returned to Europe, urging the people of England and France to follow the example of the American Revolution. In 1792 Paine published *The Rights of Man*, calling for an English Revolution to overthrow King George III and a French Revolution to overthrow King Louis XIV.

Thomas Paine wrote in 1792, *My country is the world and my religion is to do good.* Having been at the center of both the American and French Revolutions, Paine returned to America in 1802 and died in obscurity on June 8, 1809.

Selected Reading

Aldridge, Alfred O., *Man of Reason: The Life of Thomas Paine*, 1959.

Ayer, A.J., *Thomas Paine*, 1988.

Conway, Moncure D., *The Life of Thomas Paine*, 1969.

Foner, Eric, *Tom Paine and Revolutionary America*, 1976.

Williamson, Audrey, *Thomas Paine: His Life, Work, and Times*, 1973.

Fiction

Fast, Howard, *Citizen Tom Paine*, 1983.

William Penn
Right Against Tyranny
September 1670

That William Penn did with force and violence unlawfully and tu-multuously cause an assembly to riot, disturbing the peace in contempt of the King's law. **- Indictment of William Penn (1670)**

William Penn was born in London, England on October 14, 1644, the son of Admiral Sir William and Margaret (Jasper) Penn. He was a lawyer and a member of the Society of Friends, known as Quakers. In 1670 the British Parliament passed the Conventicle Act, denying all but Anglicans the freedom to worship. Upon indictment for its violation, the Act provided that the accused was to be presumed guilty unless he could prove otherwise.

On August 14, 1670, William Penn led three hundred fellow Quakers in a worship service on the street. When the authorities attempted to arrest Penn for a violation of the Conventicle Act, a minor scuffle broke out. Penn was indicted for the crime of *Unlawful and Tumultuous Assembly*. His trial began on September 1, 1670, with London's Lord Mayor Sir Samuel Starling presiding. Penn pled not guilty. His defense was to be based upon the *inalienable rights of Englishmen* granted to them by the *Magna Carta*.

During the trial, Judge Starling refused Penn the right to cross-examine or call witnesses, and repeatedly ignored or interrupted Penn when he tried speak. Starling had him tied to a chair and gagged when it was time for him to deliver his closing argument. Penn was imprisoned in London's notorious Newgate Prison while the jury deliberated. The judge instructed them to deliver a guilty verdict. They twice refused and a verdict of not guilty was recorded.

This landmark speech, *Right Against Tyranny,* is the closing speech to the jury that William Penn tried to deliver.

We have lived to an age so debauched from all humanity and reason, as well as faith and religion, that some stick not to turn butchers to their own privileges and conspirators against their own liberties. For however Magna Carta had once the reputation of a sacred unalterable law, and few were hardened enough to incur and bear the long curse that attends the violators of it, yet it is frequently objected now that the benefits there designed are but temporary, and therefore liable to alteration, as other statutes are. What game such persons play at may be read in the attempts of Dionysius, Phalaris, etc., which would have will and power be the people's law.

But that the privileges due to Englishmen by the Great Charter of England have their foundation in reason and law, and that those new Cassandrian ways to introduce will and power deserve to be detested by all persons professing sense and honesty and the least allegiance to our English Government, we shall make appear from a sober consideration of the nature of those privileges contained in that charter.

One. The ground of alteration of any law in government (where there is no invasion) should arise from the universal discommodity of its continuance, but there can be no disprofit in the discontinuance of liberty and property; therefore there can be no just ground of alteration.

Two. No one Englishman is born slave to another; neither has the one a right to inherit the sweat and benefit of the other's labor, without consent - therefore the liberty and property of an Englishman cannot reasonably be at the will and beck of another, let his quality and rank be never so great.

Three. There can be nothing more unreasonable than that which is partial, but to take away the liberty and property of any which are natural rights without breaking the law of nature (and not of will and power) is manifestly partial, and therefore unreasonable.

Four. If it be just and reasonable for men to do as they would be done by, then no sort of men should invade the liberties and properties of other men, because they would not be served so themselves.

Five. Where liberty and property are destroyed, there must always be a state of force and war, which, however pleasing it may be unto the invaders, will be esteemed intolerable by the invaded, who will no longer remain subject in all human probability than while they want as much power to free themselves as their adversaries had to enslave them; the troubles, hazards, ill consequences, and illegality of such attempts, as they have declined by the most prudent in all ages, so have they proved most uneasy to the most savage of all nations, who first or last have by a mighty torrent freed themselves, to the due punishment and great infamy of their oppressors - such being the advantage, such the disadvantage which necessarily do attend the fixation and removal of liberty and property.

We shall proceed to make it appear that Magna Carta (as recited by us) imports nothing less than their preservation,

No freeman shall be taken or imprisoned, or be disseized of his freehold, or liberties, or free customs, or be outlawed, or exiled, or any other ways destroyed; nor we will not pass upon him nor condemn him, but by lawful judgment of his peers, etc.

A freeman shall not be amerced for a small fault, but after the manner of the fault, and for a great fault after the greatness

thereof, and none of the said amercement shall be assessed, but by the oath of good and lawful men of the vicinage.

One. It asserts Englishmen to be free - that's liberty.

Two. That they have freeholds - that's property.

Three. That amercement or penalties should be proportioned to the faults committed, which is equity.

Four. That they shall lose neither, but when they are adjudged to have forfeited them, in the judgment of their honest neighbors, according to the law of the land, which is lawful judgment.

It is easy to discern to what pass the enemies of the Great Charter would bring the people.

One. They are now freemen - but they would have them slaves.

Two. They have now right unto their wives, children, and estates, as their undoubted property - but such would rob them of all.

Three. Now no man is to be amerced or punished but suitably to his fault, whilst they would make it suitable to their revengeful minds.

Four. Whereas the power of judgment lies in the breasts and consciences of twelve honest neighbors, they would have it at the discretion of mercenary judges, to which we cannot choose but add that such discourses manifestly strike at this present constitution of government; for it being founded upon the Great Charter, which is the ancient common law of the land, as upon its best foundation, none can design the canceling of the charter, but they must necessarily intend the extirpation of the English Government, for where the cause is taken away the effect must consequently cease.

And as the restoration of our ancient English laws by the Great Charter was the sovereign balsam which cured our former breaches, so doubtless will the continuation of it prove an excellent prevention to any future disturbances.

But some are ready to object that *the Great Charter consisting as well of religious as civil rights, the former having received an alteration, there is the same reason why the latter may have the like.* To which we answer that the reason of alteration cannot be the same; therefore the consequence is false. The one being a matter of opinion, about faith and religious worship, which is as various as the unconstant apprehensions of men, but the other is matter of so immutable right and justice that all generations, however differing in their religious opinions, have concentred and agreed to the certainty, equity, and indispensable necessity of preserving these fundamental laws - so that Magna Carta hath not risen and fallen with the differing religious opinions that have been in this land, but have ever remained as the stable right of every individual Englishman, purely as an Englishman. Otherwise, if the civil privileges of the people had fallen with the pretended religious privileges of the popish tyranny at the first reformation, as must needs be suggested by this objection, our case had ended here, that we had obtained a spiritual freedom, at the cost of a civil bondage, which certainly was far from the intention of the first reformers, and probably an unseen consequence, by the objectors to their idle opinion.

In short, there is no time in which any man may plead the necessity of such an action as is unjust in its own nature, which he must unavoidably be guilty of, that doth deface or cancel that law by which the justice of liberty and property is confirmed and maintained to the people. And consequently no person may legally attempt the subversion or extenuation of the force of the Great Charter. We shall proceed to prove from instances out of both.

One. Any judgment given contrary to the said charter is to be undone and holden for naught.

Two. Any that by word, deed, or counsel, go contrary to the said charter are to be excommunicated by the bishops; and the archbishop of Canterbury and York are bound to compel the other bishops to denounce sentence accordingly, in case of their remissness or neglect, which certainly hath relation to the State rather than the Church, since there was never any necessity of compelling the bishops to denounce sentence in their own case, though frequently in the people's.

Three. That the Great Charter and Charter of Forest be holden and kept in all points, and if any statute be made to the contrary, that it shall be holden for naught. . . .

Four. Another statute runs thus,

> *If any force come to disturb the execution of the common law, ye shall cause their bodies to be arrested and put in prison; ye shall deny no man right by the King's letters, nor counsel the King anything that may turn to his damage or disherison. Neither to delay right by the Great and Little Seal.*

This is the judge's charge and oath.

Such care hath been taken for the preservation of this Great Charter that . . . [it] was enacted, *That commissioners should issue forth that there should be chosen in every shire court, by the commonalty of the same shire, three substantial men, knights or other lawful, wise, and well-disposed persons, to be justices, which shall be assigned by the King's letters patent, under the Great Seal, to hear and determine without any other writ, but only their commission, such*

*plaints as shall be made upon all those that commit or offend against
any point contained in the aforesaid charters.*

So heinous a thing was it esteemed of old to endeavor an
enervation or subversion of these ancient rights and privileges that acts of Parliament themselves (otherwise the
most sacred with the people) have not been of force
enough to secure or defend such persons from condign
punishment, who, in pursuance of them, have acted inconsistent with our Great Charter. Therefore it is that great
lawyer, the Lord Coke, doth once more aggravate the example of Empson and Dudley (with persons of the same
rank) into a just caution, as well to Parliaments as judges,
justices, and inferior magistrates, to decline making or executing any act that may in the least seem to restringe or
confirm this so often avowed and confirmed Great Charter
of the liberties of England, since Parliaments are said to err
when they cross it (the obeyers of their acts punished as
time-serving transgressors) and that kings themselves
(though enriched by those courses) have, with great com-
punction and repentance, left among their dying words
their recantations.

Therefore most notable and true it was, with which we shall
conclude this present subject, what the King pleased to observe in the speech to the Parliament about 1662, namely,
The good old rules of law are our best security.

Afterward
William Penn, freed by a jury he had inspired to do justice
no matter what the cost, was released from Newgate
Prison. He went on to a life of missionary work, traveling,
writing, and speaking tirelessly on behalf of his Quaker
faith. After the death of his father, William Penn used his
inherited wealth and social position to obtain for the Quakers permission to settle in England's American colonies of

New Jersey and Delaware. Finally, in 1682, they established a colony of their own, Pennsylvania, founded on the fundamental rights of Englishmen.

In 1693 Penn, who had suffered a travesty of justice almost half his life ago, reflected on this experience and wrote, *Justice is justly represented blind, because she sees no difference in the parties concerned. She has but one scale and weight, for rich and poor, great and small. Her sentence is not guided by the person, but the cause. Impartiality is the life of justice, as is that of government.*

William Penn died on July 30, 1718.

Selected Reading

Graham, John, *William Penn*, 1916.
Hildegarde, Dolson, *William Penn, Quaker Hero*, 1961.
Janney, Samuel M., *The Life of William Penn*, 1970.
Peare, Catherine O., *William Penn: A Biography*, 1957.
Wildes, Harry, *William Penn*, 1974.

Powhatan, Chief of the Algonquins
I Know The Difference Of Peace and War
December 30, 1607

*In the cant of civilization, Powhatan, Chief of the Virginia Algon-
quins, will doubtless be branded with the epithets of tyrant and bar-
barian. But his title to greatness, though his opportunities were fewer,
is to the full as fair as that of [Mongol conquerors] Tamerlane or
Kublai Khan and several others whom history has immortalized.*
- Burk's *History of Virginia*

The Algonquin Chief Wahunsonacock (called by his people
the Great Chief of the Powhatan, and by the English settlers of Virginia *Powhatan*) was born around 1547 in a village
near present day Richmond, Virginia. Heir to his father's
small confederacy of six tribes, Wahunsonacock, after becoming Chief around 1570, added by conquest an additional twenty-four tribes to the Powhatan Nation. By 1607
this Nation extended across America's Middle Atlantic
Coast from Maryland's Eastern Shore, down Virginia's
Chesapeake Bay and Tidewater, all the way to the Carolinas.

An ancient Powhatan legend prophesied that *from the Great
Sea a Nation will arise which will destroy the Powhatan People.* The
Great Chief spent his life defending his people from the
prophesied destruction.

In May 1607 the English colony of Jamestown was established on Powhatan lands. 39 colonists had died crossing
the Atlantic. Another 73 soon died of starvation. In December 1607 Captain John Smith was ordered to lead a
party in search of Powhatan, with whom they could trade
their belongings for food. The trading party was ambushed
by a Powhatan war party. All were killed except Smith, who
was brought to the village of Werowocomoco to be judged
by Powhatan. Smith boldly offered the Great King peace or
war. The Great Chief of the Powhatan made this landmark
speech, *I Know The Difference of Peace and War.*

Captain Smith, you may understand that I, having seen the death of all my people thrice, and not one living of those three generations but myself, I know the difference of peace and war better than any in my country.

But now I am old, and ere long must die, my [three] brethren. . . , my two sisters, and their two daughters, are distinctly each other's successors; I wish their experiences no less than mine, and your love to them no less than mine to you. But [there is an old legend that from the Chesapeake Bay will arise a nation which will destroy the Algonquins and I fear] you are come to destroy my country.

[This has] so frightened all my people [that] they dare not visit [to trade with] you. What will it avail you to take [what by force] you may quietly have with love. Or to destroy them that provide you food? What can you get by war? We can hide our provisions and flee to the woods, whereby you must famish by wronging us, your friends. Why are you thus jealous of our love, seeing us unarmed, . . . willing still to feed you with what you cannot get but by our labors?

Think you I am so simple not to know it is better to eat good meat, lie well, and sleep quietly with my women and children, laugh and be merry with you, have copper, hatchets, or what I want, being your friend, than be forced to flee from all, to lie cold in the woods, feed upon acorns, roots, and such trash, and be so hunted by you that I can neither rest, eat, nor sleep; but my tired men must watch, and if a twig but break, everyone cries, *There comes Captain Smith!* Then must I fly I know not whither, and thus with miserable fear end my miserable life, leaving my pleasures to such youths as you, which through your rash unadvised [actions] may quickly as miserably end, for want of what you [will] never know how to find? Let this therefore assure you of our love and every year our friendly trade shall furnish you with corn, and now also if you would come in friendly manner to see us, and not thus with your guns and swords, as [if] to invade your foes.

Afterward

Powhatan ordered the immediate execution of John Smith. Legend says that Pocahontas, Powhatan's daughter, pleaded for Smith's life, which the Great King spared. John Smith returned empty-handed but unharmed to Jamestown. The colony, subsisting on roots, herbs, and berries, barely survived their first winter. On August 18, 1608, Captain John Smith, who had returned to England, published *A True Relation of Such Occurrences of Note that Had Happened in Virginia Since the First Planting of The Colony.* His writings made him, and Pocahontas, famous. Smith died in 1631. Pocahontas converted to Christianity in 1613 and was baptized *Rebecca.* She married Jamestown colonist John Rolfe in 1614 and died while on a visit to England in 1617.

Powhatan died in 1618. The fragile peace that kept the Jamestown Colony and the Powhatan Nation from war died with him. His younger brother, Opechancanough, became Great Chief of the Powhatan. In March 1622 the new Great Chief attempted to massacre the Jamestown Colony out of existence, killing nearly 350 colonists in a surprise attack. Opechancanough was captured and executed. By 1648, as John Smith had warned and the ancient legend had prophesied, the Powhatan Nation had been destroyed.

Selected Reading

Johnston, Charles H.L., *Famous Indian Chiefs,* 1914.
Smith, John, *A True Relation of Virginia,* 1866.
Sweetser, Kate D., *Book of Indian Braves,* 1913.

Benjamin Rush
Slave-Keeping
January 1773

*Where is the difference between the British legislator who attempts to
enslave his fellow subjects in America, by imposing taxes upon them
contrary to law and justice, and the American legislator who reduces
his African brethren to slavery, contrary to justice and humanity?*

- Benjamin Rush (1773)

Benjamin Rush was born on December 24, 1745 in Bay-
berry Township, Pennsylvania, the son of John and Susanna
(Hall) Rush. Educated at the College of New Jersey (now
Princeton University), Rush, upon his graduation at age fifteen, served a six-year apprenticeship in medicine. He pursued his medical studies in Philadelphia, Edinburgh, London, and Paris. Rush became a licensed physician in 1766
and, in the years to follow, America's leading physician. Dr.
Rush, a very rich and well respected man, volunteered much
of his time in the poorhouses, prisons, charity wards, and
mental asylums of Philadelphia. Shocked at the human misery that he found there, Rush became an outspoken, and at
times unpopular, social activist, working for reform of and
improvements in the health and well-being of poor whites,
native Americans, and, especially, African slaves.

American slavery was over 150 years old when Benjamin
Rush joined the abolitionist cause. In January 1773, the anti-
slavery Quaker faction in the Pennsylvania Assembly en-
listed Dr. Rush in a legislative attempt to stop the importation of slaves into Pennsylvania by raising taxes on slave
labor. Rush, at his own peril, agreed to add his efforts to the
fight. The result, the most famous anti-slavery statement of
colonial times, was Benjamin Rush's landmark *Address to the
Inhabitants of the British Settlements in America upon Slave-
Keeping*.

So much hath been said upon the subject of slave-keeping that an apology may be required for this address. The only one I shall offer is that the evil still continues. This may in part be owing to the great attachment we have to our own interest and in part to the subject not being fully exhausted. The design of the following address is to sum up the leading arguments against it, several of which have not been urged by any of those authors who have written upon it.

Without entering into the history of the facts which relate to the slave trade, I shall proceed to combat the principal arguments which are used to support it.

I need hardly say anything in favor of the intellects of the Negroes, or of their capacities for virtue and happiness, although these have been supposed by some to be inferior to those of the inhabitants of Europe. The accounts which travelers give us of their ingenuity, humanity, and strong attachment to their parents, relations, friends, and country, show us that they are equal to the Europeans, when we allow for the diversity of temper and genius which is occasioned by climate. We have many well-attested anecdotes of as sublime and disinterested virtue among them as ever adorned a Roman or a Christian character. But we are to distinguish between an African in his own country, and an African in a state of slavery in America. Slavery is so foreign to the human mind that the moral faculties, as well as those of the understanding, are debased and rendered torpid by it. All the vices which are charged upon the Negroes in the southern colonies and the West Indies, such as idleness, treachery, theft, and the like, are the genuine offspring of slavery, and serve as an argument to prove that they were not intended for it.

Nor let it be said in the present age that their black color (as it is commonly called) either subjects them to, or qualifies them for, slavery. The vulgar notion of their being descended from Cain, who was supposed to have been marked with this color, is too absurd to need a refutation. Without inquiring into the cause of this blackness, I shall only add upon this subject that, so far from being a curse, it subjects the Negroes to no inconveniences, but on the contrary qualifies them for that part of the globe in which Providence has placed them. The ravages of heat, diseases, and time appear less in their faces than in a white one; and when we exclude variety of color from our ideas of beauty, they may be said to possess everything necessary to constitute it in common with the white people.

It has been urged by the inhabitants of the Sugar Islands and South Carolina that it would be impossible to carry on the manufactories of sugar, rice, and indigo without Negro slaves. No manufactory can ever be of consequence enough to society to admit the least violation of the laws of justice or humanity. But I am far from thinking the arguments used in favor of employing Negroes for the cultivation of these articles should have any weight....

Now if the plantations in the islands and the southern colonies were more limited, and freemen only employed in working them, the general product would be greater, although the profits to individuals would be less, a circumstance which, by diminishing opulence in a few, would suppress luxury and vice, and promote that equal distribution of property which appears best calculated to promote the welfare of society. I know it has been said by some that none but the natives of warm climates could undergo the excessive heat and labor of the West India islands. But this argument is founded upon an error, for the reverse of this is true. I have been informed by good authority that one European who escapes the first or second year will do twice the work and live twice the number of years that an ordinary Negro man will do; nor need we be surprised at this when we hear that such is the natural fertility of soil, and so numerous the spontaneous fruits of the earth in the interior parts of Africa, that the natives live in plenty at the expense of little or no labor, which, in warm climates, has ever been found to be incompatible with long life and happiness. Future ages, therefore, when they read the accounts of the slave trade (if they do not regard them as fabulous) will be at a loss which to condemn most, our folly or our guilt, in abetting this direct violation of the laws of nature and religion.

But there are some who have gone so far as to say that slavery is not repugnant to the genius of Christianity, and that it is not forbidden in any part of the Scripture. Natural and revealed religion always speak the same things, although the latter delivers its precepts with a louder and more distinct voice than the former. If it could be proved that no testimony was to be found in the Bible against a practice so pregnant with evils of the most destructive tendency to society, it would be sufficient to overthrow its divine Original. We read it is true of Abraham's having slaves born in his house; and we have reason to believe that part of the riches of the patriarchs consisted in them; but we can no more infer the lawfulness of the practice, from the short account which the Jewish historian gives us of these facts, than we can vindicate telling a lie, because Rahab is not condemned for it in the account which is given of her deceiving the king of Jericho. We read that some of the same men indulged themselves in a plurality of wives, without any strictures being made upon their conduct for it; and yet no one will pretend to say that this is not forbidden in many parts of the Old Testament. But we are told the Jews kept the heathens in perpetual bondage. The design of

Providence in permitting this evil was probably to prevent the Jews from marrying amongst strangers, to which their intercourse with them upon any other footing than that of slaves would naturally have inclined them. Had this taken place, their national religion would have been corrupted, they would have contracted all their vices, and the intention of Providence in keeping them a distant people in order to accomplish the promise made to Abraham *that in his seed all the nations of the earth should be blessed* would have been defeated, so that the descent of the Messiah from Abraham could not have been traced, and the divine commission of the Son of God would have wanted one of its most powerful arguments to support it. But with regard to their own countrymen, it is plain, perpetual slavery was not tolerated. Hence, at the end of seven years or in the year of the jubilee, all the Hebrew slaves were set at liberty, and it was held unlawful to detain them in servitude longer than that time, except by their own consent. But if in the partial revelation which God made of his will to the Jews we find such testimonies against slavery, what may we not expect from the Gospel, the design of which was to abolish all distinctions of name and country. While the Jews thought they complied with the precepts of the law in confining the love of their neighbor *to the children of their own people*, Christ commands us to look upon all mankind (even our enemies) as our neighbors and brethren, and *in all things, to do unto them whatever we would wish they should do unto us.* He tells us further that his *Kingdom is not of this World*, and therefore constantly avoids saying anything that might interfere directly with the Roman or Jewish governments, and although he does not call upon masters to emancipate their slaves, or slaves to assert that liberty wherewith God and nature had made them free, yet there is scarcely a parable or a sermon in the whole history of his life but what contains the strongest arguments against slavery. Every prohibition of covetousness, intemperance, pride, uncleanness, theft, and murder, which he delivered, every lesson of meekness, humility, forbearance, charity, self-denial, and brotherly-love, which he taught, are leveled against this evil, for slavery, while it includes all the former vices, necessarily excludes the practice of all the latter virtues, both from the master and the slave. Let such, therefore, who vindicate the traffic of buying and selling souls seek some modern system of religion to support it, and not presume to sanctify their crimes by attempting to reconcile it to the sublime and perfect religion of the great Author of Christianity.

There are some amongst us who cannot help allowing the force of our last argument, but plead as a motive for importing and keeping slaves, that they become acquainted with the principles of the religion of our country. This is like justifying a highway robbery because part of the money acquired in this manner was appropriated to some religious use. Christianity will never be propagated by any other methods than those employed by Christ and his Apostles. Slavery is an engine as little fitted for that purpose as fire or the sword. A Christian slave is a contradiction in terms. But if we inquire into the methods employed for converting the Negroes to Christianity, we shall find the means suited to the end proposed. In many places Sunday is appropriated to work for themselves; reading and writing are discouraged among them. A belief is even inculcated amongst some that they have no souls. In a word, every attempt to instruct or convert them has been constantly opposed by their masters. Nor has the example of their Christian masters any tendency to prejudice them in favor of our religion. How often do they betray, in their sudden transports of anger and resentment (against which there is no restraint provided towards their Negroes), the most violent degrees of passion and fury! What luxury, what ingratitude, to the Supreme Being, what impiety in their ordinary conversation do some of them discover in the presence of their slaves! I say nothing of the dissolution of marriage vows, or the entire abolition of matrimony, which the frequent sale of them introduces, and which are directly contrary to the laws of nature and the principles of Christianity. Would to Heaven I could here conceal the shocking violations of chastity, which some of them are obliged to undergo without daring to complain. Husbands have been forced to prostitute their wives, and mothers their daughters to gratify the brutal lust of a master. This, all this, is practiced - Blush, ye impure and hardened wretches, while I repeat it - by men who call themselves Christians!

But further, it has been said that we do a kindness to the Negroes by bringing them to America, as we thereby save their lives, which had been forfeited by their being conquered in war. Let such as prefer or inflict slavery rather than death disown their being descended from or connected with our mother countries. But it will be found upon inquiry that many are stolen or seduced from their friends who have never been conquered; and it is plain, from the testimony of historians and travelers, that wars were uncommon among them, until the Christians who began the slave trade stirred up the different nations to fight against each other. Sooner let them imbrue their hands in each other's blood, or condemn one another to perpetual slavery, than the name of one Christian or one American be stained by the perpetration of such enormous crimes.

Nor let it be urged that by treating slaves well we render their situation happier in this country than it was in their own. Slavery and vice are connected together, and the latter is always a source of misery. Besides, by the greatest humanity we can show them, we only lessen but do not remove the crime, for the injustice of it continues the same. The laws of retribution are so strongly inculcated by the moral governor of the world that even the ox is entitled to his reward for *treading the corn*. How great then must be the amount of that injustice, which deprives so many of our fellow creatures of the just reward of their labor.

But it will be asked here, what steps shall we take to remedy this evil, and what shall we do with those slaves we have already in this country? This is indeed a most difficult question. But let every man contrive to answer it for himself.

The first thing I would recommend to put a stop to slavery in this country is to leave off importing slaves. For this purpose let our assemblies unite in petitioning the King and Parliament to dissolve the African committee of merchants. It is by them that the trade is chiefly carried on to America. We have the more reason to expect relief from an application at this juncture, as by a late decision in favor of a Virginia slave in Westminster Hall, the clamors of the whole nation are raised against them. Let such of our countrymen as engage in the slave trade be shunned as the greatest enemies to our country, and let the vessels which bring the slaves to us be avoided as if they bore in them the seeds of that forbidden fruit, whose baneful taste destroyed both the natural and moral world. As for the Negroes among us, who, from having acquired all the low vices of slavery, or who from age or infirmities are unfit to be set at liberty, I would propose, for the good of society, that they should continue the property of those with whom they grew old, or from whom they contracted those vices and infirmities. But let the young Negroes be educated in the principles of virtue and religion; let them be taught to read, and write, and afterwards instructed in some business, whereby they may be able to maintain themselves. Let laws be made to limit the time of their servitude and to entitle them to all the privileges of freeborn British subjects. At any rate let retribution be done to God and to society.

And now, my countrymen, what shall I add more to rouse up your indignation against slave-keeping? Consider the many complicated crimes it involves in it. Think of the bloody wars which are fomented by it among the African nations or, if these are too common to affect you, think of the pangs which attend the dissolution of the ties of nature in those who are stolen from their relations. Think of the many thousands who perish by sickness, melancholy, and suicide in their voyages to America. Pursue the poor devoted victims to one of the West India islands, and see them exposed there to public sale. Hear their cries, and see their looks of tenderness at each other upon being separated. Mothers are torn from their daughters, and brothers from brothers, without the liberty of a parting embrace. Their master's name is now marked upon their breasts with a red hot iron. But let us pursue them into a sugar field, and behold a scene still more affecting than this. See! the poor wretches with what reluctance they take their instruments of labor into their hands; some of them, overcome with heat and sickness, seek to refresh themselves by a little rest. But, behold, an overseer approaches them; in vain they sue for pity. He lifts up his whip, while streams of blood follow every stroke. Neither age nor sex are spared. Methinks one of them is a woman far advanced in her pregnancy. At a little distance from these behold a man who from his countenance and deportment appears as if he was descended from illustrious ancestors. Yes. He is the son of a prince and was torn by a stratagem from an amiable wife and two young children. Mark his sullen looks! Now he bids defiance to the tyranny of his master and, in an instant, plunges a knife into his heart. But let us return from this scene, and see the various modes of arbitrary punishments inflicted upon them by their masters. Behold one covered with stripes, into which melted wax is poured, another tied down to a block or a stake, a third suspended in the air by his thumbs, a fourth - I cannot relate it. Where now is law or justice? Let us fly to them to step in for their relief. Alas! The one is silent, and the other denounces more terrible punishment upon them. Let us attend the place appointed for inflicting the penalties of the law. See here one without a limb, whose only crime was an attempt to regain his liberty, another led to a gallows for stealing a morsel of bread, to which his labor gave him a better title than his master, a third famishing on a gibbet, a fourth in a flame of fire! his shrieks pierce the very heavens. O! God! where is thy vengeance! O! Humanity, Justice, Liberty, Religion! Where, where are ye fled?

This is no exaggerated picture. It is taken from real life. Before I conclude I shall take the liberty of addressing several classes of my countrymen in behalf of our brethren (for by that name may we now call them) who are in a state of slavery amongst us.

In the first place let magistrates both supreme and inferior exert the authority they are invested with in suppressing this evil. Let them discountenance it by their example, and show a readiness to concur in every measure proposed to remedy it.

Let legislators reflect upon the trust reposed in them. Let their laws be made after the spirit of religion, liberty, and our most excellent English Constitution. You cannot show your attachment to your King or your love to your country better than by suppressing an evil which endangers the dominions of the former and will in time destroy the liberty of the latter. Population, and the accession of strangers, in which the riches of all countries consist, can only flourish in proportion as slavery is discouraged. Extend the privileges we enjoy to every human creature born amongst us, and let not the journals of our assemblies be disgraced with the records of laws which allow exclusive privileges to men of one color in preference to another.

Ye men of sense and virtue, ye advocates for American liberty, rouse up and espouse the cause of humanity and general liberty. Bear a testimony against a vice which degrades human nature and dissolves that universal tie of benevolence which should connect all the children of men together in one great family. The plant of liberty is of so tender a nature that it cannot thrive long in the neighborhood of slavery. Remember the eyes of all Europe are fixed upon you, to preserve an asylum for freedom in this country, after the last pillars of it are fallen in every other quarter of the globe.

But chiefly, ye ministers of the gospel, whose dominion over the principles and actions of men is so universally acknowledged and felt, ye who estimate the worth of your fellow creatures by their immortality, and therefore must look upon all mankind as equal, let your zeal keep pace with your opportunities to put a stop to slavery. While you enforce the duties of *tithe and cummin*, neglect not the weightier laws of justice and humanity. Slavery is an Hydra sin, and includes in it every violation of the precepts of the law and the Gospel. In vain will you command your flocks to offer up the incense of faith and charity, while they continue to mingle the sweat and blood of Negro slaves with their sacrifices. If the Blood of Abel cried aloud for vengeance - if under the Jewish dispensation, cities of refuge could not screen the deliberate murderer - if even manslaughter required sacrifices to expiate it, and if a single murder so seldom escapes with impunity in any civilized country - what may you not say against that trade, or those manufactures or laws, which destroy the lives of so many thousands of our fellow creatures every year? If in the Old Testament *God swears by his holiness, and by the excellency of Jacob, that the Earth shall tremble and every one mourn that dwelleth therein for the iniquity of those who oppress the poor and crush the needy, who buy the poor with silver, and the needy with a pair of shoes,* what judgments may you not denounce upon those who continue to perpetrate these crimes, after the more full discovery which God has made of the law of equity in the New Testament. Put them in mind of the rod which was held over them a few years ago in the Stamp and Revenue Acts. Remember that national crimes require national punishments and, without declaring what punishment awaits this evil, you may venture to assure them that it cannot pass with impunity unless God shall cease to be just or merciful.

Afterward

On January 26, 1773, the Pennsylvania Assembly passed a tax measure, effectively ending the importation of slaves into their colony. On April 4, 1775, Benjamin Rush, along with Benjamin Franklin, founded the first organized anti-slavery organization, the Pennsylvania Society for Promoting the Abolition of Slavery. In 1776 Dr. Rush changed his focus from social to political reform and, as a delegate to the Second Continental Congress, signed the Declaration of Independence. In the Revolutionary War, Dr. Rush served as Surgeon General of the Army. At the end of the war, he returned to medicine, fighting against 1793's *Yellow Monster,* a yellow fever epidemic in Philadelphia that killed thousands. He also returned to social justice causes, fighting against the enslavement of millions. Dr. Rush served in 1803 as the

President of the Pennsylvania Society for Promoting the Abolition of Slavery. Rush died on April 19, 1813.

Selected Reading

Binger, Carl, *Revolutionary Doctor: Benjamin Rush*, 1966.

Corner, George W., Editor, *The Autobiography of Benjamin Rush*, 1948.

D'Elia, Donald J., *Benjamin Rush, Philosopher of the American Revolution*, 1974.

Goodman, Nathan G., *Benjamin Rush, Physician and Citizen*, 1934.

Hawke, David, *Benjamin Rush: Revolutionary Gadfly*, 1971.

Neilson, Winthrop, and Frances Neilson, *Verdict For the Doctor: The Case of Benjamin Rush*, 1958.

George Washington
Farewell Address
September 19, 1796

I, George Washington, do solemnly swear that I will faithfully execute the Office of President of the United States and will, to the best of my ability, preserve, protect, and defend the Constitution of the United States.

- Washington's Presidential Oath, April 30, 1789

George Washington was born on February 22, 1732 in Westmoreland County, Virginia, the son of Augustine Washington and Mary (Ball) Washington. Educated at home and at the College of William and Mary, Washington became, at seventeen, a licensed surveyor. He traveled extensively until 1752, when, upon the death of his older half-brother Lawrence (their father having died in 1743), he inherited the family lands, over five thousand acres.

George Washington began his military career in the French and Indian War, serving with distinction and earning promotion from Major to Brigadier General. In 1759 Washington began his political career as a member of Virginia's House of Burgesses. In 1774 he chaired the meeting that issued the revolutionary Fairfax County Resolves. One of Virginia's delegates to the First and Second Continental Congresses, George Washington was, on June 15, 1775, appointed Commanding General of the Army. At the end of the Revolutionary War, believing his military and political careers over, Washington issued two Farewell Addresses, to the Army and to the nation.

Washington was President of the Constitutional Convention and signed the Constitution. He was elected the first President of the United States. He served two terms and refused a third. His landmark speech, *The Farewell Address*, was never publicly delivered but was published in Philadelphia's *America Daily Advertiser* on September 19, 1796.

To the people of the United States, friends, and fellow-citizens, the period for a new election of a citizen to administer the Executive Government of the United States being not far distant, and the time actually arrived when your thoughts must be employed in designating the person who is to be clothed with that important trust, it appears to me proper, especially as it may conduce to a more distinct expression of the public voice, that I should now apprise you of the resolution I have formed to decline being considered among the number of those out of whom a choice is to be made.

I beg you at the same time to do me the justice to be assured that this resolution has not been taken without a strict regard to all the considerations appertaining to the relation which binds a dutiful citizen to his country - and that, in withdrawing the tender of service which silence in my situation might imply, I am influenced by no diminution of zeal for your future interest, no deficiency of grateful respect for your past kindness, but am supported by a full conviction that the step is compatible with both.

The acceptance of, and continuance hitherto in, the office to which your suffrages have twice called me, have been a uniform sacrifice of inclination to the opinion of duty, and to a deference for what appeared to be your desire. I constantly hoped that it would have been much earlier in my power, consistently with motives which I was not at liberty to disregard, to return to that retirement from which I had been reluctantly drawn. The strength of my inclination to do this, previous to the last election, had even led to the preparation of an address to declare it to you; but mature reflection on the then perplexed and critical posture of our affairs with foreign nations and the unanimous advice of persons entitled to my confidence impelled me to abandon the idea.

I rejoice that the state of your concerns, external as well as internal, no longer renders the pursuit of inclination incompatible with the sentiment of duty, or propriety, and am persuaded, whatever partiality may be retained for my services, that in the present circumstances of our country you will not disapprove my determination to retire.

The impressions with which I first undertook the arduous trust were explained on the proper occasion. In the discharge of this trust I will only say that I have, with good intentions, contributed towards the organization and administration of the government the best exertions of which a very fallible judgment was capable. Not unconscious, in the outset, of the inferiority of my qualifications, experience in my own eyes - perhaps still more in the eyes of others - has strengthened the motives to diffidence of myself; and every day the increasing weight of years admonishes me more and more that the shade of retirement is as necessary to me as it will be welcome. Satisfied that, if any circumstances have given peculiar value to my services, they were temporary, I have the consolation to believe that while choice and prudence invite me to quit the political scene, patriotism does not forbid it.

In looking forward to the moment which is intended to terminate the career of my public life, my feelings do not permit me to suspend the deep acknowledgment of that debt of gratitude which I owe to my beloved country - for the many honors it has conferred upon me - still more for the steadfast confidence with which it has supported me - and for the opportunities I have thence enjoyed of manifesting my inviolable attachment, by services faithful and persevering, though in usefulness unequal to my zeal. If benefits have resulted to our country from these services, let it always be remembered to your praise, and as an instructive example in our annals, that under circumstances in which the passions agitated in every direction were liable to mislead, amidst appearances sometimes dubious - vicissitudes of fortune often discouraging - in situations in which not unfrequently want of success has countenanced the spirit of criticism, the constancy of your support was the essential prop of the efforts and a guarantee of the plans by which they were effected. Profoundly penetrated with this idea, I shall carry it with me to the grave, as a strong incitement to unceasing vows that Heaven may continue to you the choicest tokens of its beneficence - that your union and brotherly affection may be perpetual - that the free Constitution, which is the work of your hands, may be sacredly maintained - that its administration in every department may be stamped with wisdom and virtue - that, in fine, the happiness of the people of these States, under the auspices of liberty, may be made complete by so careful a preservation and so prudent a use of this blessing as will acquire to them the glory of recommending it to the applause, the affection, and adoption of every nation which is yet a stranger to it.

Here, perhaps, I ought to stop. But a solicitude for your welfare, which cannot end but with my life, and the apprehension of danger, natural to that solicitude, urge me on an occasion like the present to offer to your solemn contemplation, and to recommend to your frequent review, some sentiments which are the result of much reflection, of no inconsiderable observation, and which appear to me all-important to the permanency of your felicity as a people. These will be offered to you with the more freedom, as you can only see in them the disinterested warnings of a parting friend who can possibly have no personal motive to bias his counsels. . . .

The unity of government which constitutes you one people is also now dear to you. It is justly so, for it is a main pillar in the edifice of your real independence, the support of your tranquillity at home, your peace abroad, of your safety, of your prosperity, of that very liberty which you so highly prize. But as it is easy to foresee that from different causes, and from different quarters, much pains will be taken, many artifices employed, to weaken in your minds the conviction of this truth - as this is the point in your political fortress against which the batteries of internal and external enemies will be most constantly and actively (though often covertly and insidiously) directed - it is of infinite moment that you should properly estimate the immense value of your national Union to your collective and individual happiness, that you should cherish a cordial, habitual, and immovable attachment to it, accustoming yourselves to think and speak of it as of the palladium of your political safety and prosperity, watching for its preservation with jealous anxiety, discountenancing whatever may suggest even a suspicion that it can in any event be abandoned, and indignantly frowning upon the first dawning of every attempt to alienate any portion of our country from the rest, or to enfeeble the sacred ties which now link together the various parts.

For this you have every inducement of sympathy and interest. Citizens by birth or choice of a common country, that country has a right to concentrate your affections. The name of American, which belongs to you in your national capacity, must always exalt the just pride of patriotism, more than any appellation derived from local discriminations. With slight shades of difference, you have the same religion, manners, habits, and political principles. You have in a common cause fought and triumphed together. The independence and liberty you possess are the work of joint councils and joint efforts - of common dangers, sufferings, and successes.

But these considerations, however powerfully they address themselves to your sensibility, are greatly outweighed by those which apply more immediately to your interest. Here every portion of our country finds the most commanding motives for carefully guarding and preserving the Union of the whole.

The North in an unrestrained intercourse with the South, protected by the equal laws of a common government, finds in the productions of the latter great additional resources of maritime and commercial enterprise, and precious materials of manufacturing industry. The South in the same intercourse, benefiting by the agency of the North, sees its agriculture grow and its commerce expand. Turning partly into its own channels the seamen of the North, it finds its particular navigation envigorated; and, while it contributes in different ways to nourish and increase the general mass of the national navigation, it looks forward to the protection of a maritime strength to which itself is unequally adapted. The East, in a like intercourse with the West, already finds, and in the progressive improvement of interior communications by land and water will more and more find, a valuable vent for the commodities which it brings from abroad or manufactures at home. The West derives from the East supplies requisite to its growth and comfort, and what is perhaps of still greater consequence, it must of necessity owe the secure enjoyment of indispensable outlets for its own productions to the weight, influence, and the future maritime strength of the Atlantic side of the Union, directed by an indissoluble community of interest as one nation. Any other tenure by which the West can hold this essential advantage, whether derived from its own separate strength, or from an apostate and unnatural connection with any foreign power, must be intrinsically precarious.

While then every part of our country thus feels an immediate and particular interest in Union, all the parts combined cannot fail to find in the united mass of means and efforts, greater strength, greater resource, proportionably greater security from external danger, a less frequent interruption of their peace by foreign nations, and, what is of inestimable value! they must derive from union an exemption from those broils and wars between themselves which so frequently afflict neighboring countries not tied together by the same government, which their own rivalships alone would be sufficient to produce, but which opposite foreign alliances, attachments, and intrigues would stimulate and embitter. Hence likewise they will avoid the necessity of those overgrown military establishments which under any form of government are inauspicious to liberty and which are to be regarded as particularly hostile to republican liberty; in this sense it is that your Union ought to be considered as a main prop of your liberty, and that the love of the one ought to endear to you the preservation of the other.

These considerations speak a persuasive language to every reflecting and virtuous mind, and exhibit the continuance of the Union as a primary object of patriotic desire. Is there a doubt whether a common government can embrace so large a sphere? Let experience solve it. To listen to mere speculation in such a case were criminal. We are authorized to hope that a proper organization of the whole, with the auxiliary agency of governments for the respective subdivisions, will afford a happy issue to the experiment. 'Tis well worth a fair and full experiment. With such powerful and obvious motives to Union affecting all parts of our country, while experience shall not have demonstrated its impracticability, there will always be reason to distrust the patriotism of those who in any quarter may endeavor to weaken its bands.

In contemplating the causes which may disturb our Union, it occurs as matter of serious concern that any ground should have been furnished for characterizing parties by geographical discriminations - Northern and Southern - Atlantic and Western - whence designing men may endeavor to excite a belief that there is a real difference of local interests and views. One of the expedients of party to acquire influence within particular districts is to misrepresent the opinions and aims of other districts. You cannot shield yourselves too much against the jealousies and heartburnings which spring from these misrepresentations; they tend to render alien to each other those who ought to be bound together by fraternal affection. The inhabitants of our Western country have lately had a useful lesson on this head. They have seen in the negotiation by the Executive, and in the unanimous ratification by the Senate, of the Treaty with Spain (and in the universal satisfaction at that event, throughout the United States), a decisive proof how unfounded were the suspicions propagated among them of a policy in the general Government and in the Atlantic States unfriendly to their interests in regard to the Mississippi. They have been witnesses to the formation of two treaties - that with Great Britain and that with Spain - which secure to them everything they could desire in respect to our foreign relations towards confirming their prosperity. Will it not be their wisdom to rely for the preservation of these advantages on the Union by which they were procured? Will they not henceforth be deaf to those advisers, if such there are, who would sever them from their brethren and connect them with aliens?

To the efficacy and permanency of your Union, a government for the whole is indispensable. No alliances however strict between the parts can be an adequate substitute. They must inevitably experience the infractions and interruptions which all alliances in all times have experienced. Sensible of this momentous truth, you have improved upon your first essay by the adoption of a Constitution of government, better calculated than your former for an intimate Union, and for the efficacious management of your common concerns. This government, the offspring of our own choice uninfluenced and unawed, adopted upon full investigation and mature deliberation, completely free in its principles, in the distribution of its powers, uniting security with energy, and containing within itself a provision for its own amendment, has a just claim to your confidence and your support. Respect for its authority, compliance with its laws, acquiescence in its measures, are duties enjoined by the fundamental maxims of true liberty. The basis of our political systems is the right of the people to make and to alter their Constitutions of government. But the Constitution which at any time exists, 'till changed by an explicit and authentic act of the whole people, is sacredly obligatory upon all. The very idea of the power and the right of the people to establish government presupposes the duty of every individual to obey the established government.

All obstructions to the execution of the laws, all combinations and associations under whatever plausible character, with the real design to direct, control, counteract, or awe the regular deliberation and action of the constituted authorities, are destructive of this fundamental principle and of fatal tendency. They serve to organize faction, to give it an artificial and extraordinary force - to put in the place of the delegated will of the Nation the will of a party - often a small but artful and enterprising minority of the community - and, according to the alternate triumphs of different parties, to make the public administration the mirror of the ill-concerted and incongruous projects of faction, rather than the organ of consistent and wholesome plans digested by common councils and modified by mutual interests. However combinations or associations of the above description may now and then answer popular ends, they are likely, in the course of time and things, to become potent engines by which cunning, ambitious, and unprincipled men will be enabled to subvert the power of the people and to usurp for themselves the reins of government, destroying afterwards the very engines which have lifted them to unjust dominion.

Towards the preservation of your government and the permanency of your present happy state, it is requisite not only that you steadily discountenance irregular oppositions to its acknowledged authority, but also that you resist with care the spirit of innovation upon its principles, however specious the pretexts. One method of assault may be to effect, in the forms of the Constitution, alterations which will impair the energy of the system, and thus to undermine what cannot be directly overthrown. In all the changes to which you may be invited, remember that time and habit are at least as necessary to fix the true character of governments as of other human institutions - that experience is the surest standard by which to test the real tendency of the existing Constitution of a country . . . ; and remember, especially, that for the efficient management of your common interests, in a country so extensive as ours, a government of as much vigor as is consistent with the perfect security of liberty is indispensable. Liberty itself will find in such a government, with powers properly distributed and adjusted, its surest guardian. It is indeed little else than a name where the government is too feeble to withstand the enterprises of faction, to confine each member of the society within the limits prescribed by the laws, and to maintain all in the secure and tranquil enjoyment of the rights of person and property.

I have already intimated to you the danger of parties in the State, with particular reference to the founding of them on geographical discriminations. Let me now take a more comprehensive view, and warn you in the most solemn manner against the baneful effects of the spirit of party generally.

This spirit, unfortunately, is inseparable from our nature, having its root in the strongest passions of the human mind. It exists under different shapes in all governments, more or less stifled, controlled, or repressed, but, in those of the popular form, it is seen in its greatest rankness and is truly their worst enemy.

The alternate domination of one faction over another, sharpened by the spirit of revenge natural to party dissension, which in different ages and countries has perpetrated the most horrid enormities, is itself a frightful despotism. But this leads at length to a more formal and permanent despotism. The disorders and miseries which result gradually incline the minds of men to seek security and repose in the absolute power of an individual; and sooner or later the chief of some prevailing faction, more able or more fortunate than his competitors, turns this disposition to the purposes of his own elevation on the ruins of public liberty.

Without looking forward to an extremity of this kind (which nevertheless ought not to be entirely out of sight), the common and continual mischiefs of the spirit of party are sufficient to make it the interest and duty of a wise people to discourage and restrain it.

It serves always to distract the public councils and enfeeble the public administration. It agitates the community with ill-founded jealousies and false alarms, kindles the animosity of one part against another, foments occasionally riot and insurrection. It opens the doors to foreign influence and corruption, which find a facilitated access to the government itself through the channels of party passions. Thus the policy and the will of one country are subjected to the policy and will of another.

There is an opinion that parties in free countries are useful checks upon the administration of the government and serve to keep alive the spirit of liberty. This within certain limits is probably true - and in governments of a monarchical cast, patriotism may look with indulgence, if not with favor, upon the spirit of party. But in those of the popular character, in governments purely elective, it is a spirit not to be encouraged. From their natural tendency, it is certain there will always be enough of that spirit for every salutary purpose, and there being constant danger of excess, the effort ought to be, by force of public opinion, to mitigate and assuage it. A fire not to be quenched, it demands a uniform vigilance to prevent its bursting into a flame lest instead of warming it should consume.

It is important likewise that the habits of thinking in a free country should inspire caution in those entrusted with its administration to confine themselves within their respective constitutional spheres, avoiding in the exercise of the powers of one department to encroach upon another. The spirit of encroachment tends to consolidate the powers of all the departments in one, and thus to create, whatever the form of government, a real despotism. A just estimate of that love of power and proneness to abuse it which predominates in the human heart is sufficient to satisfy us of the truth of this position. The necessity of reciprocal checks in the exercise of political power - by dividing and distributing it into different depositories, and constituting each the guardian of the public weal against invasions by the others - has been evinced by experiments ancient and modern, some of them in our country and under our own eyes. To preserve them must be as necessary as to institute them. If in the opinion of the people the distribution or modification of the Constitutional powers be in any particular wrong, let it be corrected by an amendment in the way which the Constitution designates. But let there be no change by usurpation, for though this, in one instance, may be the instrument of good, it is the customary weapon by which free governments are destroyed. The precedent must always greatly overbalance in permanent evil any partial or transient benefit which the use can at any time yield.

Of all the dispositions and habits which lead to political prosperity, religion and morality are indispensable supports. In vain would that man claim the tribute of patriotism who should labor to subvert these great pillars of human happiness, these firmest props of the duties of men and citizens. The mere politician, equally with the pious man, ought to respect and to cherish them. A volume could not trace all their connections with private and public felicity. Let it simply be asked, where is the security for property, for reputation, for life, if the sense of religious obligation desert the oaths which are the instruments of investigation in courts of justice? And let us with caution indulge the supposition that morality can be maintained without religion. Whatever may be conceded to the influence of refined education on minds of peculiar structure - reason and experience both forbid us to expect that national morality can prevail in exclusion of religious principle.

'Tis substantially true that virtue or morality is a necessary spring of popular government. The rule indeed extends with more or less force to every species of free government. Who that is a sincere friend to it can look with indifference upon attempts to shake the foundation of the fabric?

Promote then as an object of primary importance institutions for the general diffusion of knowledge. In proportion as the structure of a government gives force to public opinion, it is essential that public opinion should be enlightened.

As a very important source of strength and security, cherish public credit. One method of preserving it is to use it as sparingly as possible - avoiding occasions of expense by cultivating peace, but remembering also that timely disbursements to prepare for danger frequently prevent much greater disbursements to repel it - avoiding likewise the accumulation of debt, not only by shunning occasions of expense, but by vigorous exertions in time of peace to discharge the debts which unavoidable wars may have occasioned, not ungenerously throwing upon posterity the burden which we ourselves ought to bear. The execution of these maxims belongs to your representatives, but it is necessary that public opinion should cooperate. To facilitate to them the performance of their duty, it is essential that you should practically bear in mind that towards the payment of debts there must be revenue - that to have revenue there must be taxes - that no taxes can be devised which are not more or less inconvenient and unpleasant - that the intrinsic embarrassment inseparable from the selection of the proper objects (which is always a choice of difficulties) ought to be a decisive motive for a candid construction of the conduct of the Government in making it, and for a spirit of acquiescence in the measures for obtaining revenue which the public exigencies may at any time dictate.

Observe good faith and justice towards all nations. Cultivate peace and harmony with all. Religion and morality enjoin this conduct, and can it be that good policy does not equally enjoin it? It will be worthy of a free, enlightened, and (at no distant period) a great nation, to give to mankind the magnanimous and too novel example of a people always guided by an exalted justice and benevolence. Who can doubt that in the course of time and things, the fruits of such a plan would richly repay any temporary advantages which might be lost by a steady adherence to it? Can it be that Providence has not connected the permanent felicity of a nation with its virtue? The experiment at least is recommended by every sentiment which ennobles human nature. Alas! is it rendered impossible by its vices?

In the execution of such a plan nothing is more essential than that permanent, inveterate antipathies against particular nations and passionate attachments for others should be excluded, and that in place of them just and amicable feelings towards all should be cultivated. The nation which indulges towards another an habitual hatred or an habitual fondness is in some degree a slave. It is a slave to its animosity or to its affection, either of which is sufficient to lead it astray from its duty and its interest. Antipathy in one nation against another disposes each more readily to offer insult and injury, to lay hold of slight causes of umbrage, and to be haughty and intractable, when accidental or trifling occasions of dispute occur. Hence frequent collisions, obstinate, envenomed and bloody contests. The nation promoted by ill-will and resentment sometimes impels to war the government, contrary to the best calculations of policy. The government sometimes participates in the national propensity, and adopts through passion what reason would reject; at other times, it makes the animosity of the nation subservient to projects of hostility instigated by pride, ambition, and other sinister and pernicious motives. The peace often, sometimes perhaps the liberty, of nations has been the victim.

So likewise a passionate attachment of one nation for another produces a variety of evils. Sympathy for the favorite nation, facilitating the illusion of an imaginary common interest in cases where no real common interest exists, and infusing into one the enmities of the other, betrays the former into a participation in the quarrels and wars of the latter, without adequate inducement or justification; it leads also to concessions to the favorite nation of privileges denied to others, which is apt doubly to injure the nation making the concessions by unnecessarily parting with what ought to have been retained, and by exciting jealousy, ill-will, and a disposition to retaliate, in the parties from whom equal privileges are withheld; and it gives to ambitious, corrupted, or deluded citizens (who devote themselves to the favorite nation), facility to betray, or sacrifice the interests of their own country, without odium, sometimes even with popularity - gilding with the appearances of a virtuous sense of obligation, a commendable deference for public opinion, or a laudable zeal for public good - the base or foolish compliances of ambition, corruption, or infatuation.

As avenues to foreign influence in innumerable ways, such attachments are particularly alarming to the truly enlightened and independent patriot. How many opportunities do they afford to tamper with domestic factions, to practice the arts of seduction, to mislead public opinion, to influence or awe the public councils! Such an attachment of a small or weak, towards a great and powerful nation, dooms the former to be the satellite of the latter.

Against the insidious wiles of foreign influence, I conjure you to believe me, follow-citizens, the jealousy of a free people ought to be constantly awake, since history and experience prove that foreign influence is one of the most baneful foes of republican government. But that jealousy to be useful must be impartial, else it becomes the instrument of the very influence to be avoided instead of a defense against it. Excessive partiality for one foreign nation and excessive dislike of another cause those whom they actuate to see danger only on one side, and serve to veil and even second the arts of influence on the other. Real patriots, who may resist the intrigues of the favorite, are liable to become suspected and odious, while its tools and dupes usurp the applause and confidence of the people to surrender their interests.

The great rule of conduct for us in regard to foreign nations is, in extending our commercial relations, to have with them as little political connection as possible. So far as we have already formed engagements, let them be fulfilled with perfect good faith. Here let us stop.

Europe has a set of primary interests which to us have none or a very remote relation. Hence she must be engaged in frequent controversies, the causes of which are essentially foreign to our concerns. Hence therefore it must be unwise in us to implicate ourselves by artificial ties in the ordinary vicissitudes of her politics or the ordinary combinations and collisions of her friendships or enmities.

Our detached and distant situation invites and enables us to pursue a different course. If we remain one people, under an efficient government, the period is not far off when we may defy material injury from external annoyance, when we may take such an attitude as will cause the neutrality we may at any time resolve upon to be scrupulously respected. When belligerent nations, under the impossibility of making acquisitions upon us, will not lightly hazard the giving us provocation, when we may choose peace or war as our interest guided by our justice shall counsel.

Why forego the advantages of so peculiar a situation? Why quit our own to stand upon foreign ground? Why, by interweaving our destiny with that of any part of Europe, entangle our peace and prosperity in the toils of European ambition, rivalship, interest, humor, or caprice?

'Tis our true policy to steer clear of permanent alliances with any portion of the foreign world - so far, I mean, as we are now at liberty to do it - for let me not be understood as capable of patronizing infidelity to existing engagements (I hold the maxim no less applicable to public than to private affairs that honesty is always the best policy). I repeat it therefore - let those engagements be observed in their genuine sense. But in my opinion it is unnecessary and would be unwise to extend them.

Taking care always to keep ourselves, by suitable establishments, on a respectably defensive posture, we may safely trust to temporary alliances for extraordinary emergencies.

Harmony, liberal intercourse with all nations, are recommended by policy, humanity, and interest. But even our commercial policy should hold an equal and impartial hand. . . . There can be no greater error than to expect or calculate upon real favors from nation to nation. 'Tis an illusion which experience must cure, which a just pride ought to discard.

In offering to you, my countrymen, these counsels of an old and affectionate friend, I dare not hope they will make the strong and lasting impression I could wish - that they will control the usual current of the passions, or prevent our nation from running the course which has hitherto marked the destiny of nations. But if I may even flatter myself that they may be productive of some partial benefit, some occasional good - that they may now and then recur to moderate the fury of party spirit, to warn against the mischiefs of foreign intrigue, to guard against the impostures of pretended patriotism - this hope will be a full recompense for the solicitude for your welfare by which they have been dictated.

How far in the discharge of my official duties I have been guided by the principles which have been delineated, the public records and other evidences of my conduct must witness to you and to the world. To myself, the assurance of my own conscience is that I have at least believed myself to be guided by them.

In relation to the still subsisting war in Europe, my proclamation of the 22nd of April, 1793 is the index to my plan. Sanctioned by your approving voice and by that of your representatives in both Houses of Congress, the spirit of that measure has continually governed me - uninfluenced by any attempts to deter or divert me from it.

After deliberate examination with the aid of the best lights I could obtain, I was well satisfied that our country, under all the circumstances of the case, had a right to take, and was bound in duty and interest to take, a neutral position. Having taken it, I determined, as far as should depend upon me, to maintain it with moderation, perseverance, and firmness.

The considerations which respect the right to hold this conduct, it is not necessary on this occasion to detail. I will only observe that, according to my understanding of the matter, that right, so far from being denied by any of the belligerent powers, has been virtually admitted by all.

The duty of holding a neutral conduct may be inferred, without anything more, from the obligation which justice and humanity impose on every nation, in cases in which it is free to act, to maintain inviolate the relations of peace and amity towards other nations.

The inducements of interest for observing that conduct will best be referred to your own reflections and experience. With me, a predominant motive has been to endeavor to gain time to our country to settle and mature its yet recent institutions, and to progress without interruption to that degree of strength and consistency which is necessary to give it, humanly speaking, the command of its own fortunes.

Though, in reviewing the incidents of my administration, I am unconscious of intentional error, I am nevertheless too sensible of my defects not to think it probable that I may have committed many errors. Whatever they may be, I fervently beseech the Almighty to avert or mitigate the evils to which they may tend. I shall also carry with me the hope that my country will never cease to view them with indulgence, and that after forty-five years of my life dedicated to its service with an upright zeal, the faults of incompetent abilities will be consigned to oblivion, as myself must soon be to the mansions of rest.

Relying on its kindness in this as in other things, and actuated by that fervent love towards it which is so natural to a man who views in it the native soil of himself and his progenitors for several generations, I anticipate with pleasing expectation that retreat (in which I promise myself to realize, without alloy, the sweet enjoyment of partaking) in the midst of my fellow-citizens, the benign influence of good laws under a free government, the ever favorite object of my heart, and the happy reward, as I trust, of our mutual cares, labors, and dangers.

Afterward

George Washington's last official act was his attendance, on March 4, 1797, at the Inauguration of John Adams. He retired to Mount Vernon, dying there on December 14, 1799.

Washington's first biographer, Reverend Mason Locke *Parson* Weems, began to embellish Washington's life when he published, in 1800, *The Life of George Washington: With Curious Anecdotes, Equally Honorable to Himself and Exemplary to His Young Countrymen*, with this famous passage, *"George,"* said his father, *"do you know who killed that beautiful little cherry tree yonder in the garden?" Looking at his father with the sweet face of youth, brightened with the inexpressible charm of all-conquering truth, young George Washington bravely cried out, "I cannot tell a lie, Pa. I did it with my little hatchet."* Abraham Lincoln, writing in 1842, knew that Washington's life needed no embellishments - *To add brightness to the sun, or glory to the name of Washington, is alike impossible. Let none attempt it. In solemn awe pronounce the name, and in its naked deathless splendor, leave it shining on.*

Selected Reading

Borden, Morton, Compiler, *George Washington*, 1969.
Callahan, North, *George Washington, Soldier and Man*, 1972.

Cunliffe, Marcus, *George Washington, Man and Monument*, 1958.

Harrison, Maureen, and Steve Gilbert, Editors, *George Washington: Word For Word*, 1998.

McCann, Alfred W., *Greatest of Men, Washington*, 1927.

Weems, Mason L., *A History of the Life and Death, Virtues & Exploits of General George Washington*, 1927.

Roger Williams
The Twelve Tenets Of Conscience
1644

I present for your eyes and hearts this discourse of blood, of the bloody tenets of persecution, oppression, and violence, in the cause and matters of conscience. **- Roger Williams (1644)**

The Puritans founded the Massachusetts Bay Colony in 1630 as a theocracy, a state using its secular power to enforce Church laws and to ensure worship of the official state religion. On February 9, 1631, they welcomed a new immigrant to Massachusetts Bay Colony, the Reverend Roger Williams. Williams had been born in London, England about 1603, the son of James and Alice (Pemberton) Williams. He was educated in religion at Cambridge University and by the time of his arrival had earned the reputation of *a godly minister.*

Williams' welcome was to be short-lived. He was offered the pulpit of Boston Church, the most important Congregational Church in the Bay Colony. In an act of conscience he refused. Williams was a *Separatist,* believing in separation of church and state and religious liberty. He turned his back on Boston and began to preach in Plymouth and Salem. Speaking from the pulpit and writing to the public, Williams continued to criticize the Puritan government. On October 9, 1635, the Puritan government and the Puritan clergy struck back. Williams was charged, tried, and found guilty of harboring *new and dangerous* religious opinions. He was banished from the Massachusetts Bay Colony. Roger Williams went on to found a colony at Providence, Rhode Island, where church and state were separate and religious liberty was encouraged.

This landmark statement of Roger Williams' beliefs, *The Twelve Tenets Of Conscience,* is drawn from his famous 1644 work, *The Bloody Tenets of Persecution.*

First, that the blood of so many hundred thousand souls of Protestants and Papists, spilt in the wars of present and former ages for their respective consciences, is not required nor accepted by Jesus Christ, the Prince of Peace.

Second, pregnant scriptures and arguments are throughout the work proposed against the doctrine of persecution for cause of conscience.

Third, satisfactory answers are given to scriptures, and objections produced by Mr. Calvin, Beza, Mr. Cotton, and the ministers of the New English churches and others former and later, tending to prove the doctrine of persecution for cause of conscience.

Fourth, the doctrine of persecution for cause of conscience is proved guilty of all the blood of the souls crying for vengeance under the altar.

Fifth, all civil states with their officers of justice in their respective constitutions and administrations are proved essentially civil, and therefore not judges, governors, or defenders of the spiritual or Christian state and worship.

Sixth, it is the will and command of God that (since the coming of his Son, the Lord Jesus) a permission of the most paganish, Jewish, Turkish, or antichristian consciences and worships be granted to all men in all nations and countries; and they are only to be fought against with that sword which is only (in soul matters) able to conquer, to wit, the sword of God's Spirit, the Word of God.

Seventh, the state of the Land of Israel, the kings and people thereof in peace and war, is proved figurative and ceremonial, and no pattern nor precedent for any kingdom or civil state in the world to follow.

Eighth, God requireth not a uniformity of religion to be enacted and enforced in any civil state, which enforced uniformity (sooner or later) is the greatest occasion of civil war, ravishing of conscience, persecution of Christ Jesus in his servants, and of the hypocrisy and destruction of millions of souls.

Ninth, in holding an enforced uniformity of religion in a civil state, we must necessarily disclaim our desires and hopes of the Jew's conversion to Christ.

Tenth, an enforced uniformity of religion throughout a nation or civil state confounds the civil and religious, denies the principles of Christianity and civility, and that Jesus Christ is come in the flesh.

Eleventh, the permission of other consciences and worships than a state professeth only can (according to God) procure a firm and lasting peace (good assurance being taken according to the wisdom of the civil state for uniformity of civil obedience from all forts).

Twelfth, lastly, true civility and Christianity may both flourish in a state or kingdom, notwithstanding the permission of divers and contrary consciences, either of Jew or Gentile. . . .

Afterward

In *The Bloody Tenets of Persecution for the Cause of Conscience*, from which *The Twelve Tenets of Conscience* are drawn, Roger Williams advocated both religious tolerance and the complete separation of church and state, anticipating by well over one hundred years Thomas Jefferson's *Virginia Statute of Religious Freedom* (1779), James Madison's *Memorial Against Religious Assessments* (1785), George Washington's *Letter to the Hebrew Congregation of Newport, Rhode Island* (1790) and the

First Amendment's Free Exercise and Establishment Clauses (1791).

Roger Williams, colonial America's first great advocate of democratic government and religious freedom, went on to found and lead New England's first religiously tolerant democratic colony, the Providence Plantations, in present day Rhode Island. He died there in 1683. Three hundred years after his trial and banishment, the Commonwealth of Massachusetts rescinded his sentence.

Selected Reading

Brockunier, Samuel, *The Irrepressible Democrat: Roger Williams*, 1940.

Carpenter, Edmund J., *Roger Williams: A Study of the Life, Times and Character of a Political Pioneer*, 1909.

Covey, Cyclone, *The Gentle Radical: Roger Williams*, 1966.

Chupack, Henry, *Roger Williams*, 1969.

Easton, Emily, *Roger Williams: Prophet and Pioneer*, 1969.

Eaton, Jeanette, *Lone Journey: The Life of Roger Williams*, 1944.

Ernst, James Emanuel, *Roger Williams, New England Firebrand*, 1969.

Garrett, John, *Roger Williams, Witness Beyond Christendom*, 1970.

Straus, Oscar S., *Roger Williams, the Pioneer of Religious Liberty*, 1894.

John Winthrop
The "Little Speech" On Liberty
July 3, 1645

We cannot part from our native country without much sadness of heart and many tears in our eyes.
- John Winthrop's "Farewell To England" (1630)

On March 29, 1630, nearly seven hundred English Puritans, members of a non-conformist sect seeking a place where they could practice their *purer form of worship* without the interference of the Anglican Church or the English Government, began their Atlantic crossing to found a colony in New England. Their leader was John Winthrop.

John Winthrop was born on January 12, 1588 in Edwardston, England, the son of Adam and Anne (Brown) Winthrop. Educated at Cambridge University, he became a lawyer and a Puritan. The Puritans were a barely tolerated religious minority. In the late 1620's, Winthrop began to plan a Puritan migration to the *Promised Land* - America.

John Winthrop served as a multi-term Governor of the Massachusetts Bay Colony. During his long tenure in office, no dissent from the state's religiously inspired political processes and the Church's civilly protected religious practices was tolerated. Winthrop banished opponents who disagreed with him on religious matters. He bullied opponents who disagreed with him on secular matters. In October 1644, his political opponents struck back. He was accused of making an arbitrary decision in a minor legal dispute in favor of his political followers - an impeachable offense which would, in effect, banish him from power. John Winthrop brilliantly defended himself at the impeachment trial held before the Massachusetts General Court. This landmark speech, which he would later call the *"Little Speech" On Liberty*, was delivered after his acquittal on July 3, 1645.

John Winthrop

I suppose something may be expected from me upon this charge that has befallen me, which moves me to speak now to you; yet I intend not to intermeddle in the proceedings of the court or with any of the persons concerned therein. Only I bless God that I see an issue of this troublesome business. I also acknowledge the justice of the court, and for mine own part I am well satisfied. I was publicly charged, and I am publicly and legally acquitted, which is all I did expect or desire. And though this be sufficient for my justification before men, yet not so before the God who hath seen so much amiss in my dispensations (and even in this affair) as calls me to be humble.

For to be publicly and criminally charged in this court is matter of humiliation (and I desire to make a right use of it), notwithstanding I be thus acquitted. If her father had spit in her face (saith the Lord concerning Miriam), should she not have been ashamed seven days? Shame had lien upon her, whatever the occasion had been. I am unwilling to stay you from your urgent affairs, yet give me leave (upon this special occasion) to speak a little more to this assembly. It may be of some good use to inform and rectify the judgments of some of the people, and may prevent such distempers as have arisen among us.

The great questions that have troubled the country are about the authority of the magistrates and the liberty of the people. It is yourselves who have called us to this office, and, being called by you, we have our authority from God, in way of an ordinance, such as hath the image of God eminently stamped upon it, the contempt and violation whereof hath been vindicated with examples of divine vengeance.

I entreat you to consider that when you choose magistrates, you take them from among yourselves, men subject to like passions as you are. Therefore, when you see infirmities in us, you should reflect upon your own, and that would make you bear the more with us, and not be severe censurers of the failings of your magistrates, when you have continual experience of the like infirmities in yourselves and others.

We account him a good servant who breaks not his covenant. The covenant between you and us is the oath you have taken of us, which is to this purpose, that we shall govern you and judge your causes by the rules of God's laws and our own, according to our best skill. When you agree with a workman to build you a ship or house, etc., he undertakes as well for his skill as for his faithfulness, for it is his profession, and you pay him for both. But when you call one to be a magistrate he doth not profess or undertake to have sufficient skill for that office, nor can you furnish him with gifts, etc., therefore you must run the hazard of his skill and ability. But if he fail in faithfulness, which by his oath he is bound unto, that he must answer for. If it fall out that the case be clear to common apprehension, and the rule clear also, if he transgress here, the error is not in the skill, but in the evil of the will - it must be required of him. But if the case be doubtful, or the rule doubtful, to men of such understanding and parts as your magistrates are, if your magistrates should err here, yourselves must bear it.

For the other point concerning liberty, I observe a great mistake in the country about that. There is a twofold liberty - natural (I mean as our nature is now corrupt) and civil or federal. The first is common to man with beasts and other creatures. By this man, as he stands in relation to man, simply hath liberty to do what he lists; it is a liberty to evil as well as to good. This liberty is incompatible and inconsistent with authority and cannot endure the least restraint of the most just authority. The exercise and maintaining of this liberty makes men grow more evil, and in time to be worse than brute beasts. . . . This is that great enemy of truth and peace, that wild beast, which all the ordinances of God are bent against, to restrain and subdue it.

The other kind of liberty I call civil or federal; it may also be termed moral, in reference to the covenant between God and man in the moral law, and the politic covenants and constitutions among men themselves. This liberty is the proper end and object of authority, and cannot subsist without it; and it is a liberty to that only which is good, just, and honest. This liberty you are to stand for, with the hazard (not only of your goods, but) of your lives, if need be. Whatsoever crosseth this is not authority, but a distemper thereof. This liberty is maintained and exercised in a way of subjection to authority; it is of the same kind of liberty wherewith Christ hath made us free. The woman's own choice makes such a man her husband; yet, being so chosen, he is her lord, and she is to be subject to him, yet in a way of liberty, not of bondage; and a true wife accounts her subjection her honor and freedom, and would not think her condition safe and free but in her subjection to her husband's authority. Such is the liberty of the church under the authority of Christ, her king and husband; his yoke is so easy and sweet to her as a bride's ornaments; and if, through forwardness or wantonness, etc., she shake it off at any time, she is at no rest in her spirit until she take it up again; and whether her lord smiles upon her, and embraceth her in his arms, or whether he frowns, or rebukes, or smites her, she apprehends the sweetness of his love in all, and is refreshed, supported, and instructed by every such dispensation of his authority over her. On the other side, ye know who they are that complain of this yoke and say, let us break their bands, etc., we will not have this man to rule over us.

Even so, brethren, it will be between you and your magistrates. If you stand for your natural corrupt liberties, and will do what is good in your own eyes, you will not endure the least weight of authority, but will murmur, and oppose, and be always striving to shake off that yoke; but if you will be satisfied to enjoy such civil and lawful liberties, such as Christ allows you, then will you quietly and cheerfully submit unto that authority which is set over you, in all the administrations of it, for your good. Wherein, if we fail at any time, we hope we shall be willing (by God's assistance) to hearken to good advice from any of you, or in any other way of God; so shall your liberties be preserved, in upholding the honor and power of authority among you.

Afterward
John Winthrop, the twelve-time Governor of the Massachusetts Bay Colony, died on March 26, 1649.

Selected Reading
Morgan, Edmund, *The Puritan Dilemma*, 1958.
Raymer, Robert, *John Winthrop*, 1963.
Winthrop, John, *The History of New England, 1630-1649*, 1825.

EXCELLENT BOOKS ORDER FORM

(Please xerox this form so it will be available to other readers.)

Please send
Copy(ies)

_____ of LANDMARK AMERICAN SPEECHES:
     VOL. I: THE 17TH & 18TH CENTURIES @ $17.95
_____ of LANDMARK AMERICAN SPEECHES:
     VOL. II: THE 19TH CENTURY @ $17.95
_____ of LANDMARK AMERICAN SPEECHES:
     VOL. III: THE 20TH CENTURY @ $17.95
_____ of LANDMARK DECISIONS I @ $17.95
_____ of LANDMARK DECISIONS II @ $17.95
_____ of LANDMARK DECISIONS III @ $17.95
_____ of LANDMARK DECISIONS IV @ $17.95
_____ of LANDMARK DECISIONS V @ $17.95
_____ of LANDMARK DECISIONS VI @ $17.95
_____ of SCHOOLHOUSE DECISIONS @ $17.95
_____ of LIFE, DEATH, AND THE LAW @ $17.95
_____ of OBSCENITY & PORNOGRAPHY DECISIONS @ $17.95
_____ of FREEDOM OF SPEECH DECISIONS @ $17.95
_____ of FREEDOM OF THE PRESS DECISIONS @ $17.95
_____ of FREEDOM OF RELIGION DECISIONS @ $17.95
_____ of THE MURDER REFERENCE @ $17.95
_____ of THE RAPE REFERENCE @ $17.95
_____ of ABORTION DECISIONS: THE 1970's @ $17.95
_____ of ABORTION DECISIONS: THE 1980's @ $17.95
_____ of ABORTION DECISIONS: THE 1990's @ $17.95
_____ of CIVIL RIGHTS DECISIONS: 19th CENTURY @ $17.95
_____ of CIVIL RIGHTS DECISIONS: 20th CENTURY @ $17.95
_____ of THE ADA HANDBOOK @ $17.95

Name: _____

Address: _____

City: _____ State: _____ Zip: _____

Add $1 per book for shipping and handling.
California residents add sales tax.
OUR GUARANTEE: Any Excellent Book may be returned at any
time for any reason and a full refund will be made.

Mail your check or money order to: Excellent Books,
Post Office Box 131322, Carlsbad, California 92013-1322
Phone: 760-598-5069/Fax: 240-218-7601/E-mail: xlntbks@aol.com
Internet Address: EXCELLENTBOOKS.COM